OPEN
CHURCH
HISTORY OF AN IDEA
by
Esther Barnhart McBride

;

Cover: Saint Peter's Church
         Citicorp Center
         New York City

Printer: Starline Creative Printing
         Albuquerque, New Mexico

To my husband Jewel—

    a workingman with abundant fellow-feeling for the poor, the unemployed, and all the victims of human misery . . .

    who spent his working years along the waterfront, rubbing elbows with all sorts and conditions of men and women . . .

    and who, amid the dust and din of life, found Jesus Christ and abides in fellowship with our Lord and Savior.

CONTENTS

PREFACE

In 1974, Saint Peter's Lutheran Church on Manhattan's East Side in New York City, founded in 1861, tore down its old Gothic building, sold the air rights over its property to a bank, and announced plans for "the World's First Condominium Church," to house a children's theater, an art gallery, a visitors center, and a day care center. Ralph E. Peterson, who had been pastor of Saint Peter's since 1966, explained that he wanted to turn his church into an "urban living room" that would be open day and night. "It's always been my dream to have an open church," he said. "Being open makes you vulnerable, but when you're vulnerable, people take care of you."[1]

Peterson's "urban living room" became a reality in 1977, when the present building, designed as a "majestic rock, a stable monument which affirms God's presence in the heart of the City," was dedicated. The public throng of humanity that daily populate the Citicorp Center, of which Saint Peter's is now a part, pause, one and all, to look down into a beautiful sunken sanctuary and to contemplate the back side of the magnificent organ, bared to public view as one turns the corner at 54th Street and Lexington Avenue. In addition to the sanctuary there is a 250-seat theater, a music room and a studio located on the lower level—all "acoustically treated and available for cultural events sponsored by the congregation."[2] Just inside the public entrance hangs a handsome plaque testifying that "the Municipal Art Society of New York honors St. Peter's Lutheran Church for providing our city with a congregation of amenities that give delight to both body and soul."

The congregation lists as its ministers the People of Saint Peter's Church. "We are here," they say, "to serve the Lord and the people of New York City. Our new building was dedicated in the confidence that in symbol and function our church home would reflect our heavenly vision and serve as an urban center of mission and prayer. . . . Worship is central each day as we celebrate God's love and renew our Christian life. As we reach out to the city, we offer a full program of music including jazz, chamber music, choral works, instrumental and vocal recitals."[3]

Saint Peter's outreach to the City includes, among other activities, a Breakfast Feeding Program, on Tuesday mornings, for the homeless and the hungry, and Sundays on the Terrace in the summer, combining adult forums with traditional vacation church school for children. Saint Peter's shares the Breakfast Feeding Program with Saint Bartholomew's Church on Park Avenue, where "volunteers have been helping other churches and synagogues open their doors to the homeless in the hope that there will soon be a place for a free meal in the midtown area every day of the week."[4]

The remarkable "urban living room" that has risen to towering heights at 54th and Lexington in New York City marks the culmination of a "total reversal of tradition" in American Lutheranism that became apparent in the 1960s. Urban Lutheran congregations, large and small, engaged in a new aggressiveness marked by social activism, community service, and "evangelism beyond the traditional clienteles." Many churches opened their doors to provide weekday social service programs for school dropouts, destitute elderly, preschool minority children, or refugees from Uganda. Other churches monitored city elections, sponsored drug treatment centers and migrant worker projects, or provided instruction in guitar and saxophone.[5]

In Pennsylvania, in 1973, churches offered their facilities in a new program of community treatment centers for former prison inmates and provided scholarships "for city police and firemen in appreciation of their services to the church." In Baltimore, churches made their buildings available to the city school system for parent education programs.[6]

Mainstream American Protestantism in general, in fact, was characterized in the 1960s by "accelerating accommodation" to the nonreligious culture. Secularism came to be celebrated as—not the enemy of the churches—but rather "the true realization of the churches' faith."[7] The idea of churches wide open to the secular culture, however, is not new to American Protestantism. In the joining together of Saint Bartholomew's with Saint Peter's, for example, to provide a breakfast feeding program for the homeless, there can be discerned a connection to a significant number of urban "free and open" churches that flourished in American cities a century ago.

Saint Bartholomew's was one of a group of pioneer Episcopalian churches that abolished pew rents and staffed their buildings with doctors, athletic directors, charity organization workers, and home economics teachers in elaborate efforts to reach the unchurched urban masses and to diminish the distance between rich and poor in American cities by merging the well-to-do "uptown" congregation with the "city mission" of the tenements.

Alongside of Saint Bartholomew's was the Church of the Holy Communion, reported to be the first free church in America and the first to be opened for daily services; the Galilee Mission of Calvary Parish, with its unique Olive Tree Inn and Restaurant; and St. George's, which, although a rich church spending over a hundred thousand dollars annually, with an endowment fund of twice that amount, was also a "frontier" church, facing that "pitiful wilderness of human life below 14th Street," working "not by proxy and at long range, but at first hand and within its own precincts."[8]

The Gothic building that was once the Church of the Holy Communion still stands intact, in its exterior, at the corner of Sixth Avenue and West Twentieth Street in New York City. It was deconsecrated in 1971, but it can never be torn down, as it has been designated a historical landmark (as has the J. Pierpont Morgan home on Madison Avenue, now the New York headquarters of the Lutheran Church in America). The interior of this landmark church building now represents, symbolically, secularism in the extreme. It is being transformed into a Limelight Entertainment Complex, with "champagne rooms," banquet halls, a restaurant, a dance floor on a hydraulic lift, and spiral staircases.[9]

The Gothic structure "was a church. But it's not a church anymore," notes John Carmen, public relations director for the transformation. "It's the only church in

Manhattan that was for sale,'' explains Peter Gatien, the thirty-year-old self-made millionaire who bought the church building in 1983. ''The architecture is outstanding. Very few buildings have ever been put together as well.''[10]

Gatien claims, rightly perhaps, that he is saving a landmark that was wasting away from neglect. He plans to use the original pews, the stained glass windows, the altar, and the solid marble floor. ''It may be a nightclub but it'll be a fine place,'' Carmen declares. ''When this church is finished this block is gonna glow.''[11]

What, then, has happened to the Church of the Holy Communion? Does the conversion to the Limelight Entertainment Complex represent the demise of this famous ''church of beginnings,'' the church that established the first ''fresh air'' work in the city of New York, the first employment society for poor women, and the first Anglican sisterhood in America?[12]

The Church of the Holy Communion, fortunately, has not disappeared. Today, it is bound together with Calvary Church and St. George's Church in a combined parish endeavor housed at St. George's and including, among other programs, a day care center, a ministry to the deaf, and a neighborhood thrift shop. These remarkable Episcopalian congregations are still ministering to ''that pitiful wilderness of human life below 14th Street.''

Thus the ''open church'' idea in American Protestantism now has more than a century of history. Out of the pioneer work of the open churches of a century ago came, for example, the Open and Institutional Church League, organized in 1894 by a group of New York pastors. The League sought to abolish ''so far as possible the distinction between the religious and the secular,'' and to sanctify ''all days and all means to the great end of saving the world for Christ.''[13]

The ''free and open'' churches viewed themselves as ''institutions'' that ministered seven days a week to the physical and spiritual wants of all people within their reach. These churches sponsored clinics, free Saturday night concerts, self-supporting restaurants and lodging houses, woodyards for the unemployed, ''fresh air work'' for women and children, and ''gold-cure establishments'' for drunkards. There was a marked emphasis on practical education. Institutional churches sponsored libraries and literary societies and carried on kindergartens, trade schools, and community colleges. Bethany College and Beacon College in Philadelphia, Plymouth Institute in Indianapolis, and Temple University were among the schools that grew out of the institutional church movement.

The newer methods of the free and open churches found expression in all parts of the country, in many forms. Berkeley Temple in Boston offered evening classes in dressmaking, stenography, millinery, painting, elocution, and languages. The People's Palace of New Jersey had a capacious amusement hall providing billiards for twenty cents an hour; pool for three cents a cue; and bagatelle, crokinole, quoits, and thirty different kinds of small games, absolutely free. Judson Memorial Baptist in lower New York financed its manifold educational, missionary, and philanthropic work with endowment income from an apartment house built in architectural harmony with the church. The more aggressive free and open churches engaged in municipal reform activity through Sabbath Leagues, Law and Order Leagues, and such well-known reform groups as the City Vigilance League of New York City and the Civic Federation of Chicago.[14]

Toward the end of the century, however, the clergy and laity of the institutional churches turned away from secularistic activities and municipal reform to return to the ''old-time religion'' of moral preaching and personal regeneration. Protestant progressives concluded that the business of the church was not to be all things to all people, and not to wield the civil power, but rather to interpret God to a nation "that can but does not worship."[15]

Twentieth century American Protestantism has just completed a cycle very similar to that performed by the free and open churches of the late nineteenth century. The activistic turmoil in Protestant churches in the late 1960s produced a "widening gap" between church leadership and the man in the pew and "plunged the church into its most serious crisis of credibility in recent history." Visiting Christians from other lands expressed alarm at the "new intimacy with the national culture" they sensed in American churches. Early in 1975, a diverse group of eighteen Christian theologians gathered at the Hartford Seminary Foundation issued an "unprecedented document" strongly affirming traditional Christian teachings and calling for an end to Christian "captivity" to "fads, cultural idols, and the dictates of 'modern thought.'" Sociologist Peter Berger warned that "the American state was not conceived in a secularist mode" and that "the loss of spirit in our religious institutions has serious implications for other aspects of American life." He concluded that the social aggressiveness of American Protestantism in the 1960s was a "misadventure" that might bring "a new seriousness about the theological content of mainstream Protestantism."[16]

In other words, there is an ebb and flow in the "open church" idea in American Protestantism. This historical account of the free and open churches of the late nineteenth and early twentieth centuries is herewith presented to provide American Protestants and social do-gooders with a perspective and, hopefully, to help all of us understand how Americans get caught up, from time to time, in the "periodical psychic sprees"[17] that are characteristic of American reform and American Protestantism. At the same time, the history of these earlier free and open churches provides a remarkable documentary of the vitality, genuine social concern, and "Americanness" of this country's Protestant churches. American Christianity has never been divorced from social problems and public affairs, and the free and open churches have borne testimony, and will continue to bear testimony to that enormously important fact.

Esther Barnhart McBride
Rio Rancho, New Mexico
July 1983

NOTES

1. Gay Nagle, "The Divine Condominium," *Sky,* Sept. 1974. Peterson left St. Peter's in 1981 and now resides in Guilford, Connecticut.

2. A complete description of the building and its symbolism is available to the public in printed material distributed by St. Peter's. These quotations are taken from "Saint Peter's Church, 4/6/82."

3. Ibid.

4. Saint Peter's Church, "Breakfast Feeding Program: An Opportunity to Help the Homeless."

5. The quotations are taken from Peter Berger, "Battered Pillars of the American System: Religion," *Fortune,* Apr. 1975. See also, for example, Carl T. Uehling, "Politics and Healing and Friendly Visitors," *Lutheran,* 3 Oct. 1973; and Edgar R. Trexler, "New Life through Music," ibid., 5 Dec. 1973.

6. Armin G. Weng, "Ministering All Year Long," *Lutheran,* 16 Oct. 1974; and William E. Diehl, "447 Walnut," ibid., 10 July 1974.

7. Berger, "Battered Pillars." See also Harvey Cox, *The Secular City: Secularization and Urbanization in Theological Perspective* (London, 1965).

8. The quotations are from Henry C. Bourne, "Four Institutional Churches. I. St. George's, New York," *Congregationalist,* 13 Apr. 1893; and Frank Mason North, "New Era of Church Work in the City of New York," *Christian City* 9 (1897): 8.

9. See Susan Mulcahy, "The Congregation Will Please Dance," New York *Post,* 8 Feb. 1983.

10. James Sheehan, "High Tech Nightspot Rises Where Worshippers Prayed," *Chelsea Clinton News,* 28 Apr. 1983.

11. Ibid.

12. See "Fifty Years of Beginnings," *Outlook,* 19 Dec. 1896.

13. "Platform of the Open and Institutional Church League," *Open Church* 1 (1897): 4.

14. See George Willis Cooke, "The Institutional Church," *New England Magazine* 14 (1896): 645-660.

15. Shailer Mathews, "The Christian Church and Social Unity," *American Journal of Sociology* 5 (1900): 456-469.

16. Berger, "Battered Pillars," and "Theological Group Affirms Faith in Traditional Christian Concepts," *Lutheran,* 5 Mar. 1975. For the text of the original Hartford appeal and essays by eight of its principal architects, see Peter L. Berger and Richard John Neuhaus, eds., *Against the World for the World: The Hartford Appeal and the Future of American Religion,* Crossroad Edition (New York, 1976).

17. Richard Hofstadter, *Age of Reform,* Vintage Edition (n.d., reprinted from New York, 1955), p. 17.

CHAPTER ONE

Renegade Calvinists and New Puritans: The Rise of the Orthodox Social Gospel 1865-1880

The transitional period in American history between the Civil War and the First World War brought profound changes to America in its industrial life, its intellectual life, and its religious life. Urbanization was of a twofold nature. Immigration itself was "part of a European move from farm to city—an Irish or Polish farm to an American city." But native Americans also moved from farm to city, especially in the Middle West. "By the end of the century, Chicago was the nation's second largest city, with rapid growth notable in Detroit, Milwaukee, Minneapolis, St. Paul, Indianapolis, Cleveland, Columbus, Toledo, Kansas City, and Omaha."[1]

The greatest revolution, perhaps, was in the labor market, where "thousands of propertyless men traded only their skills and their sweat." In the last quarter of the century, however, the intellectual and religious scenes were also in turmoil. Developments in historiography and sociology toppled long-accepted "God-given laws" of economics and political science. The appearance of such new disciplines as anthropology, archeology, and psychology brought men everywhere to radical new concepts of the nature of man and the function of government and social organizations. The solidarity of mankind became "a favorite teaching of the day," and the social thought of Herbert Spencer became "an integral part of the mental equipment of every educated man." It was a period characterized by "the growing acceptance of evolution as a guide in all departments of thought," and by a striving for the "scientific habit of mind, . . . a general readiness to connect cause and event, to ask *why* and *whence* and *for what* in respect to all things."[2]

American Protestants had varying reactions to the great rush of industrial, social, and intellectual ferment and change that swept the country in the last quarter of the nineteenth century. Some felt that the old doctrines of Puritan individualism and "fixed laws of society" were in "grave . . . incongruity and conflict with the living reason and moral consciousness of the world" and therefore could not be reconciled with the new teachings of humanism, brotherhood, and evolution. Theology seemed, in fact, to be replacing economics as the "dismal science." The old, tried methods of preaching and church worship no longer seemed to work. "The church is being gradually engulfed by a sandwave," lamented New York pastor Edward Judson. "All that the angel Gabriel himself could do would be to retard the process of decay."[3]

1

Alert Protestant thinkers, however, sensitive to the great variety of social forces that pressed for attention in the new cosmopolitan environment, surveyed the broad spectrum of American Protestantism and found in it historical strands and indigenous trends that seemed equal to a new, modern, diversified ministry and theology. Using a new-found sense of history, they took a fresh look at Christianity as a religion that had grown out of New Testament social conditions marked by highly organized and densely populated urban societies enjoying the refinements of a complex civilization. They thereby found a new faith in Christianity as a religion "possessing the quality of modernity, and adapted to the needs of the modern world." The essence of Christianity was sufficient to the task, but many adjustments would have to be made.[4]

Protestant preachers, in general, adjusted to the new times. Up until the 1840s Protestant preaching had been doctrinal—"as it mainly ought to be," declared liberal Congregationalist Theodore T. Munger in 1884. The minister had put all specific sins into "one vast sin—an infinite thing demanding infinite punishment." No man had ability; some were "elected"; all were summoned to repentance.

"Such, in general, was the framework of the preaching of the last generation," wrote Munger in 1884. "It was honestly believed; it was urged often with great skill and power. . . . It served a purpose and did its work [but] it was blind to the nature and the end of man [and] it broke almost more hearts than it healed."[5]

After the Civil War—the culmination of the slavery question, a moral issue that brought permanent cleavages in many Protestant denominations—preaching became more social. There was a marked shift from the "other world" to this world. The "social conscience" became a major concern of the times. The church became a more definitely philanthropic organization. "Regeneration, conversion, atonement, sacrifice, all took on a new meaning, and became, so to speak, socialized; 'election' became avowedly an election for service, not for personal salvation; salvation came to include the reconstruction of human society into a kingdom of God on earth."[6]

A "school of progressive orthodoxy" thus appeared that effectively combined new doctrines with remnants of the old. It added to the old doctrine of God's sovereignty a new theological recognition of the lordship of Jesus Christ in the human world. It emphasized a new, positive conception of man and taught that human beings could participate in the work of redeeming mankind. By 1895 progressive orthodoxy was well represented in denominational and interdenominational organizations, in several seminaries, and in some of the most influential pulpits. It boasted a variety of thought and method, a mature theology, virile federations for mutual support, and effective leadership. It eventually inherited the name Social Gospel, although it represented the moderate, rather than the radical, segments of the larger movement that bore the name.[7]

Critics complained that "preachers became lecturers of moral reform; pulpits became lyceum platforms; churches became social clubs." Orthodoxy's Social Gospel was, nevertheless, a "reformatory and inspirational" humanitarian movement that left its permanent mark on American Protestantism and extended its influence to civic and political circles beyond the church. The movement was a socializing of American Puritanism; it was also a return to the organic, collectivistic, and altruistic emphases of original Calvinism. It was appropriately described, by some, as "the new puritanism."[8]

Henry Churchill King, president of Oberlin College, noted, for example, that progressive orthodoxy had kept the "four great positives" of the older puritanism—a sense of God as "the realest of all realities"; a sense of divine calling, mission, and message; a deep sense of responsibility and accountability; and a "tremendous sense of the significance and value of life." King suggested that the new puritanism consisted of adding to these "the great positives of the modern spirit"—the scientific sense of unity and growth, the psychological emphasis upon the breadth and complexity of human life, the modern convictions of the unity of man, and "the social consciousness, with its deep sense of the sacredness of the individual person."9

The orthodox Social Gospel—or "orthodox social Christianity," as its own leaders preferred to call it—was, in fact, a vigorous and influential facet of a theological revolution that has been called, by some historians, America's "third great awakening." The first awakening had centered about Jonathan Edwards and George Whitefield; the second, about Charles Grandison Finney. The third, extending from 1875 to 1915, was similar to the first two in that "a theological and ecclesiastical reorientation coincided with an intellectual and social reorientation in such a way as to awaken a new interest in the Christian ethos," and to produce "significant alterations in the definition of that ethos and its relationship to American life."10

That orthodox social Christianity was indeed part of such a "great awakening" is evidenced by the variety of people who participated in it, and by by the breadth and diversity of their sundry individual activity. Washington Gladden and William S. Rainsford were the representative clergymen of orthodox social Christianity. Berkeley Temple in Boston and St. George's in New York were its representative churches; Andover, its representative seminary; Horace Bushnell, its primal source; Walter Rauschenbusch and Shailer Mathews, its theologians; Josiah Strong, its organizer; Francis Greenwood Peabody, its philosopher and academician; William Jewett Tucker, its educator; Charles Richmond Henderson, its leading sociologist and social technician; Richard T. Ely, its leading economist; Graham Taylor, its civic leader; Henry George, its politician; Charles H. Parkhurst, its municipal reformer; J.H.W. Stuckenberg, its historian, and Lyman Abbott, its journalist. The real heroes of the movement, however, were the laity of dozens of Protestant congregations—the first true "priesthood of all believers" in American Protestantism—the Brothers of St. Andrew and the King's Daughters, the friendly visitors of the charity organization societies, the courageous women of the white ribbon, and "stewards of wealth," such as J. Pierpont Morgan.

The social Christianity that became prominent in America after the Civil War was not so much a radical shift in American Protestantism from Calvinistic theocracy to nonsectarian humanism as it was a reflowering of the Protestant hope for a unified Christian commonwealth. The Puritan Separatists of New England had sought to realize this hope by creating a perfect Christian commonwealth untainted by the world, in which church and state were united as one and in which "morality laws buttressed the religious code." When social and political developments in America made union of church and state untenable, early stewards of wealth (such as Arthur and Lewis Tappan, Lyman Beecher, William E. Dodge, and Theodore Frelinghuysen) had sought, through their wealth and influence, "to make people conform to a particular Protestant interpretation of the gospel." With "keen urgency," through whatever avenues open to them, these "trustees of God" used a dual method of making all men "good": moral suasion and political action.11

Following the Civil War, militant Protestants continued their traditional methods of moral suasion through temperance agitation, revivals, and rescue missions. Alongside of these, however, appeared a new phenomenon: the so-called "institutional church," conceived as a "free and open church" that would embrace all classes and conditions of men and thus eventually bring to fruition the democratic Christian commonwealth so patiently and so optimistically sought after by American Protestants.

The "institutional church" was the creation of liberal socially minded Protestants who considered democratic education, rather than moral suasion, to be the most effective way to mold the American nation into the kingdom of God. The principle of evangelism through education, in fact, received widespread acceptance by orthodox Protestants, largely as a result of the dramatic impact of the theology of Horace Bushnell upon American Protestantism. Bushnell—an original thinker, an imaginative preacher and theologian, and an "internal innovator" who belonged "half to the mystics and half to science, and wholly to himself"—did more than any other single American Protestant after Jonathan Edwards to "reduce the distance between sinful man and perfect God."[12]

In 1838, in an unsigned article entitled "The Spiritual Economy of Revivals of Religion," published in the *Quarterly Christian Spectator,* Bushnell suggested "Christian nurture" as an alternative to revivalism. In his *Christian Nurture,* published in 1846, he sought to establish the proposition that "the child is to grow up a Christian, and never know himself as being otherwise"—a very simple statement, but it shook New England theology "to its foundations" and "compelled the church to acknowledge that there must be growth from within as well as conquest from without if she was to hold her rightful possessions as well as extend her boundaries."[13]

Bushnell was born in Connecticut in 1802. His mother had been reared in the Episcopalian church, but both parents became members of the Congregational church. By the time Bushnell entered Yale College in 1823, "unbelief" had come to be his "element," and throughout his lifetime he remained "conversant with the various types of unbelief" that appeared upon the American scene in rapid succession. He carried on, for example, an extensive correspondence with O.A. Bartel of Boston, "a catholic-minded man of genius, who represented the more spiritual side of Unitarianism."[14]

Out of a "sense of responsibility for others," Bushnell was ordained pastor of the North Church in Hartford in 1833. In his Hartford pulpit he spoke against slavery and the spoils system and preached sermons that were "ethical treatises on the nature and function of government." He held to the Puritan conception of the state as moral. He agreed with Unitarian theologian William Ellery Channing that "social barriers and distinctions, insofar as they restrict sympathy, and substitute the spirit of caste . . . for the spirit of humanity" were "gross violations of the Christian law." Bushnell noted that "gamblers, drunkards, thieves, prostitutes, and the victims of these evils were not in the pew in any number"; he concluded that there was not enough "realism in religion." He saw a need for a socialized Christianity, in which men would "lay hold of each other in some fellow-feeling, and fulfill answering conditions of social benefit." Bushnell was the childhood pastor of child welfare pioneer Charles Loring Brace, and his influence upon Washington Gladden, Lyman Abbott, and numerous other well-known Social Gospel clergymen was to be profound.[15]

In *Christian Nurture* Bushnell stoutly defended the idea that "the *force-principle* in every shape is to be discarded." His admonition was heeded by every Protestant revivalist and evangelist that followed him. Evangelist Dwight L. Moody, for example, substituted the "inquiry room" for Finney's "anxious seat," thus paving the way for the more indirect psychological methods of persuasion used by such twentieth century revivalists as Billy Sunday and Billy Graham. Bushnell's theme that "the soul of all improvement is the improvement of the soul" also became the rationale for the "institutional church" movement, with its optimistic belief in the spiritual use of all forms of betterment of human life.[16]

It was, however, a renegade Anglican clergyman—William S. Rainsford—who created the empirical human welfare agency that came to be known as the "institutional church." In his exciting autobiography *Story of a Varied Life,* Rainsford described himself as "poorly fitted to be the rector of a great parish in a great city." He explained, "I was inexperienced, very imperfectly educated, and had little knowledge of the world. Many of those I was thrown with disagreed radically with me."[17]

This "poorly fitted" man, however, devoted twenty-four years to building, at St. George's Episcopal Church in New York City, the best and most widely known model of a "free and open" church. J. Pierpont Morgan and Seth Low (successively mayor of Brooklyn, resident of Columbia College, and mayor of New York) were members of his vestry. His work on the East Side brought him the close friendship of Jacob Riis. He called Terence V. Powderly, the much vilified leader of the Knights of Labor, "as brave and unselfish a worker for the public good as I ever met." Theodore Roosevelt was another close friend.

Rainsford had spent his childhood in Dundalk, Ireland, where in church the Sunday morning collection was gathered in long copper spoons; where "the pews . . . were of different sizes, . . . some . . . large and square, even having a table, and sometimes a stove, in the middle." Rainsford's father had been a leader among the Puritan Evangelicals, who under the leadership of Whitefield and Wesley had "saved the cause of real religion in England" in the eighteenth century by "preaching on the streets and in the cottages of the poor." In his autobiography, Rainsford was later to praise the nineteenth century Evangelical protest against "the worldliness, ignorance, and supineness of the national church," but he also concluded that the Evangelical party in England had shared in a "universal failure" when it "turned a deaf ear to the exceeding bitter cry of Labour."

Rainsford's family moved to London in 1865. An illness took him to southern France. He returned home in 1868, intent upon passing the competitive examination for a commission in the Royal Artillery. There came a sudden intervention in this plan, when a friend of his took him to a little Baptist chapel off Mile End Road on the East Side of London. There his friend unexpectedly asked him to speak to a group of poor mothers gathered together in a sewing class.

"How I got on my feet I don't know," Rainsford later wrote in his autobiography. When he looked at their "worn gray faces," he "fumbled the pages" of his pocket Bible and "gasped and muttered something." He "never found a text"; and when "no help, no light, . . . no coherent word" came to him, he sat down. Some of them pitied him and cried, as he made his way to the door, "Come back and speak to us again next Tuesday."

As Rainsford walked home alone, a "new resolve" came to him to go back the next week, and "stand in that poor little chapel and speak to those burdened folk." The following week he faced "that roomful of mothers" again. "Before I knew it," he wrote later, "I had forgotten W.S.R. entirely, and I was talking, not to the poor draggled bonnets or the mass of wan faces beneath them, but to human souls looking at me out of human eyes." He became "a weekly fixture" at Miss Logan's sewing class.

In 1869, Rainsford and a friend escorted an emigrant band from the Mile End congregation to Canada. They roamed the Indian country "from sea to sea" and Rainsford returned to a London with "no beauty anywhere" and a Cambridge that was "a disappointment." He had seen a new land where "poverty was not a necessity," and "everyone had a chance." By contrast, East London was "infinitely depressing"—no free space, no greenery, no playground, and only "a dirty smoke-laden pall."

Without any seminary training, in 1874 Rainsford went from Cambridge directly to his first parish, at St. Giles in the old city of Norwich. He decided on the method of street revival preaching. He discovered Mazzini's writings and read Matthew Arnold's poetry, but later recorded that his "first growing pain" came from studying the New Testament itself. Then he experienced his "Pentecost" in a revivalistic retreat lead by Dwight L. Moody, visiting from America, and Adolph Monod, "a charming, cultivated, saintly French Hugenot." Rainsford felt that he must leave England for a time. "It hurts dreadfully to change your idea of God," he wrote later, "but if you do not, he will surely fade out of your life altogether."

In a strenuous two-year period of tent preaching and "missions" in New York, Baltimore, Philadelphia, and Ontario, Rainsford found everywhere men and women "anxious to speak about their doubts and troubles, and trying to get in touch with God." He concluded, however, that "a mission cannot save a failing church." He came to realize that "what we failed to see was that men and women who came of tainted stock, conceived in sin and cradled in dirt, . . . could not get saved at all." He gradually formed for himself an evolutionary approach to the Christian religion, in which "the God of the supernatural must fade, replaced by the God of things as they are."

In 1878 Rainsford answered a call to St. James Cathedral Church in Toronto, where he spent "perhaps the best four years" of his life as assistant rector to a dean in failing health. At first, at St. James, he experienced "undeniable failure." Attendance and collections began to fall off. To the "old Evangelicals" he "smelt of heresy," and the "stand-bys" of the church "began to protest and sometimes to go to other churches." Then Rainsford began "to feel a new courage, to cease to dread anything, even [his] own doubts." He "discovered Fiske" and "rediscovered Mazzini," and the "larger liberty and light" he had won for his own soul bound him and his people together in a "new warm companionship."

In the midst of a deadlock between the Cathedral vestry and the bishop that followed upon the death of the dean, Rainsford left St. James for St. George's, where he faced "an empty church and an empty treasury, and a vast, unchurched population . . . to be won." In Toronto he had come to the belief that the church of God "should be a teaching house and a dancing house; a reading house and a playing house; and because it was these, it should be a preaching house." He aimed to fashion "a great free church, open to all, not in name only, not by profession only, but in actual operation." At St. George's from the beginning, he insisted upon a policy that would call upon church members "to surrender their property rights in their pews." He envisioned "a church of the people, a truly democratic church"—one place "besides the grave" where all men might have a "common right," and might be shown "the way to all sorts of betterment."

The essential principles that Rainsford stood for in accepting the call to St. George's took shape in what came to be called the "institutional church." As time went on, "it was copied, and sometimes misrepresented and misunderstood," but it deserves discussion and study as an innovative, living, human welfare mechanism that left its permanent mark on Protestant evangelism in America, and on American education and the profession of social work.[18]

NOTES

1. The quotations are from Edwin Scott Gaustad, *A Religious History of America* (New York, 1966), p. 227.

2. The quotations are from Gaustad, *A Religious History,* p. 227; F.D. Hoskins, "Pauperism and Its Treatment," *American Church Review* 31 (1879): 135; Franklin H. Giddings, "The Relation of Social Theory to Public Policy," *American Journal of Sociology* 16 (1911): 579; and Theodore T. Munger, "Recent Changes in Christian Thought," *Outlook,* 27 Feb. 1892.

3. The quotations are from T.M. Post, "Transition Periods in Religious Thought," *Andover Review* 1 (1884): 583; "Washington Gladden," *Outlook,* 27 Jan. 1906; and Judson, "Symposium on the Institutional Church. VI. The Institutional Church a Remedy for Social Alienation," *Homiletic Review* 33 (1897): 473.

4. The quotation is from "Salvation Social," *Independent,* 27 Oct. 1910.

5. Munger, "Then and Now," *Independent,* 29 May 1884.

6. "Washington Gladden."

7. The term Social Gospel "did not become general until about 1910" (Henry F. May, *Protestant Churches and Industrial America* [1963, reprinted from New York, 1949], p. 170fn). The name's origin is attributed to the *Social Gospel,* a magazine published by George Davis Herron's Christian Commonwealth Colony in Georgia. For a thorough and reliable treatment of George D. Herron, W.D.P. Bliss, and other liberal and radical exponents of the Social Gospel, see Charles Howard Hopkins, *Rise of the Social Gospel in American Protestantism, 1865-1900* (New Haven, 1940), pp. 173-200. Hopkins presents the Social Gospel as an indigenous response of American Protestantism to the challenge of a new industrial society, reflecting realistic efforts of Protestant clergymen to meet crisis conditions in their parishes.

8. The quotations are from "Washington Gladden."

9. *The Twenty-fifth Anniversary of the Commencement of the Pastorate of Rev. Washington Gladden, D.D. over the First Congregational Church of Columbus, Ohio, 1882-1907: Sermon and Addresses,* pp. 45, 46 (Graham Taylor Collection, Newberry Library, Chicago).

10. See William G. McLoughlin, *Modern Revivalism: Charles Grandison Finney to Billy Graham* (New York, 1959), pp. 8-10, from which the quotations are taken. Perry Miller differs from McLoughlin in delineating a "great Awakening of 1857 and 1858," which "was different from all previous revivals," in that "it was concentrated in the cities"; stressed prayer rather than preaching; "arose from below, among the laity"; and "confirmed the union of the millennial expectation" with business and applied science *(The Life of the Mind in America: From the Revolution to the Civil War* [New York, 1965], pp. 88-91).

11. For a lively account of the political activities of the Protestant "trustees of God" and their "benevolent societies," see Clifford S. Griffin, *Their Brothers' Keepers: Moral Stewardship in the United States, 1800-1865* (New Brunswick, 1960), from which the quotations are taken.

12. The quotations are from May, *Protestant Churches and Industrial America,* p. 84; and Theodore T. Munger, *Horace Bushnell: Preacher and Theologian* (Boston, 1899), p. 156.

13. The quotations are from McLoughlin, *Modern Revivalism,* pp. 149, 150; Munger, *Horace Bushnell,* p. 67; and Francis E. Clark, "A Quarter-Century of Christian Endeavor," *Outlook,* 5 Jan. 1906.

14. Munger, *Horace Bushnell,* pp. 21, 135; and "Horace Bushnell: A Memorial Sermon Preached in the Chapel of Yale College, Sunday, 26 March 1876," *New Englander* 36 (1877): 158.

15. Munger, *Horace Bushnell,* passim; Channing, "Address on Temperance at request of the Council of Mass. Temperance Society, Oden, Boston, 28 Feb. 1837" *(Works of William E. Channing, D.D.* [8th complete ed., Boston, 1848], Vol. 2, pp. 301-341); Gordon A. Riegler, *Socialization of the New England Clergy, 1800-1860* (Greenfield, 1945), p. 3; and Gladden, *Recollections* (Boston, 1909), pp. 119, 164-167.

16. The quotations are from A.S. Cresebrough, "The Theological Opinions of Horace Bushnell as Related to His Character and Christian Experience," *Andover Review* 6 (1886): 128; and S. Parkes Cadman, "The Advance Movement of the Church in Great Cities," *Christian City* 9 (1897): 282. See also McLoughlin, *Modern Revivalism,* pp. 166-281, 400-529.

17. Rainsford, *Story of a Varied Life: An Autobiography* (New York, 1922), p. 5.

18. Rainsford, *Story of a Varied Life,* passim.

CHAPTER TWO

Being All Things to All People:
America's Free and Open Churches
1875-1900

The appearance of "free and open" churches in American cities and towns in the last quarter of the nineteenth century was the resounding answer of American Protestantism to the problem of the "vast lapsed masses . . . who seldom darken the door of a church." In 1885 the Reverend George F. Pentecost of Brooklyn, New York, warned, "Let us recognize the facts of the case. The Church is not reaching the masses: the masses are not drawn to the Church. There is a great gulf betwixt the two, and it is becoming 'a great gulf fixed.' . . . We must first recognize the existence of the gulf before we will think of bridging it."[1]

The gulf between the church and the masses had already been noted by some Protestant clergymen in the 1870s. In 1873 one clergyman had called the churches "religious club rooms, where four or five hundred favored disciples of Jesus can meet and be entertained . . . while the common people who loved Him so when he was on earth and would love Him so now could they only have Him revealed to them, are rambling in the streets outside, or sunning themselves on the wharves and the Common."[2]

In the 1880s Protestant pastors and laymen became increasingly concerned because the growth of churches in the cities was rapidly falling behind the increase in population. In 1885, Pentecost noted that the churches were not keeping pace with the population growth in Brooklyn, Philadelphia, St. Louis, Chicago, or Cincinnati. In 1889 another clergyman pointed out the new phenomenon of the "downtown" church, where the "family constituency" had moved away, "leaving in the vicintage a fluctuating population made up largely of clerks, young married people with small incomes, and others in moderate circumstances,—the classes from which are to come the future businessmen of the city." A Baptist clergyman in New York concluded from the federal census of 1890 that, out of a male population of nine hundred thousand in New York City, only about three percent were Protestant.[3]

Pentecost correctly noted that the lapsed masses were not all of one class and condition. They included "the poor of all classes," but also "the middle and upper ten thousand." They included "the second generation of foreigners, whose parents were Romanists," and also, significantly, "the laboring classes."[4] American workingmen, in general, felt a deep and bitter alienation from the Christian church. They believed that American Protestant clergymen catered only to capitalists, aristocrats, and rich men, and ignored and even condemned common laborers, who in all likelihood were living on the brink of poverty, in wretched conditions.[5]

The alienation of workingmen from the church was an important aspect of the long and sometimes bloody struggle of American labor to achieve social and economic recognition. The constant, unchanging cry that motivated the agitation and organization of labor in the United States in the nineteenth century, and even into the twentieth, was, "Let us have security in order that we might become men."[6]

THE RISE OF LABOR

The rise of organized labor, a movement reflecting the longings of laboring men and women for "that better life," was a salient feature of the nineteenth century in America. Before the Civil War, labor unions had existed only in the form of local guilds. Starting in 1832, however, local unions in New England had begun to band together for labor reform aimed at improving working conditions and achieving wage levels that would permit the purchase of "the necessaries of life." Agitation of the New England Workingman's Association led to the first Industrial Congress of the United States in 1845, but labor unions of national scope did not appear until after the Civil War.[7]

Efforts of laboring men and women to organize for their own betterment met with fierce opposition from employers, from churches, and from the public in general. All looked with fear upon the workingman as "foreign born" and upon laboring groups as a whole as "the dangerous classes."[8] Some of the earlier trade unions, as a result, were organized in the form of secret societies and under the title of friendly societies and mutual benefit clubs, because "in no other way would public sentiment permit them to exist."[9] The United States Congress provided for the incorporation of labor organizations as early as 1866, but even as late as 1895 few labor organizations had availed themselves of the provisions of this act, preferring to agitate independently, often with rampant use of strikes and violence and with utter disregard for public sentiment or even public safety.

From the beginning, the labor movement in America was plagued by factions and jealousies; however, there were elements within it that strived consistently to achieve unity within the entire movement. The *Workingman's Advocate,* the official organ of the Knights of St. Crispin, for example, continually pleaded for labor unity in order to achieve desired legislative goals. "Upon one platform" declared this journal as early as 1871, "all the industrial classes of the country can stand, and find their interest in one organization. . . . The first great need of workingmen is to get rid of unworthy suspicions, of jealousies."[10]

To further the aim of labor unity, the *Advocate* backed the Declaration of Principles adopted first at the National Labor convention held in Chicago in 1867 and ratified at every national convention thereafter, as the platform that would win for workingmen the control of the government. This Declaration of Principles reached its full expression as the "Platform of the National Industrial Congress, Adopted April 16, 1874," and had as its corollary the 1872 platform of the National Labor party. The Declaration demanded, among other things, the establishment of a Bureau of Labor Statistics, the establishment of cooperative institutions, the reserving of public lands for the people, the adoption of measures providing for the health and safety of those engaged in mining, manufacturing, and building; a law to compel chartered corporations to pay their employees at least once a month, the abolition of the contract system on national, state, and municipal works; a system of public markets and cheap transportation, the substitution of arbitration for strikes, the prohibition of the importation of all servile races, the enactment and enforcement of equitable apprentice laws, the abolishment of the system of contracting the labor of convicts, and the reduction of hours of labor to eight hours per day. These Principles represented, in general, the concrete demands of American workingmen in the last half of the nineteenth century.[11]

ALIENATION FROM THE CHURCH

Almost all urban workingmen were agreed on another important point. They had been forced to the common conclusion that the comfortable church life of the average pew occupant in any American urban congregation was grossly inconsistent with the life and ministry of the Jesus Christ of the New Testament. Many thoughtful clergymen were keenly aware of this indictment, and of the realities of American church life that had provoked it, but concluded reluctantly that bridging the gulf between the church and the workingman was an impossible task. "The complexities of social life, and the adaptation to all classes of different styles of Christian work, offer problems that seem to me past the ingenuity of any man or set of men, or perhaps any one generation, successfully to solve," wrote one in 1890.[12]

Some clergymen viewed the alienation of workingmen from the church as only one symptom of the vastly larger problem of the relationships between the rich and the poor, and the relationships between capital and labor—problems that formed a great part of the "Social Question" as viewed by Protestants. In 1884, for example, influential Congregationalist Washington Gladden sent a circular to 250 workingmen from his church in Columbus, Ohio. From the answers he received, he concluded that workingmen "cannot see that the Christian law of love is doing much to mitigate Ricardo's 'iron law of wages'," and that "the feeling that arises from the present conflict between employers and employees . . . is the bottom fact of the workingman's alienation from the church."[13]

For many, contemplating the Social Question brought only a feeling of panic and a sense of impending revolution. In 1886 the Reverend Frederic Dan Huntington, Protestant Episcopal bishop of central New York, called "the subject of the mutual duties of the richer and the poorer" a "moral" question, and lamented that the problem was too diversified, the interests "too much mixed," and "the energies of pure selfishness . . . too obstinate, to encourage . . . any adjustment." Pentecost called the "heathen" population of large cities "infidel and godless"; and Professor M.H. Richards, of Muhlenberg College in Allentown, Pennsylvania, cried that "we cannot afford to coquet with 'higher criticism' and such like theological 'fads' while this Hannibal is at our gates. . . . The revolution in which we are found is one which permits no one to be an idle spectator; everyone becomes sooner or later a participant."[14]

Gladden was one of the few clergymen who dared to suggest that the Christian church had a God-given role to help solve the Social Question. He arranged meetings between capital and labor at his church in Columbus; and even before that, in 1880, the Reverend J.H. Rylance, rector of St. Mark's Church in New York, had delivered four lectures in his church on competition, communism, cooperation, and socialism. Rylance singled out cooperation as "the best human solution of the problem of the relationships of capital and labor, especially if entered upon in the kindly and honest spirit" of the Christian religion.[15]

Several years later, in New Haven, a group of workingmen approached the Reverend Newman Smyth of Center Church and asked him to discuss labor problems from his pulpit, having been attracted by Smyth's incidental references to social problems. Smyth responded by delivering a series of sermons, in which he declared that workingmen had come to look upon Christianity "almost with the enmity . . . toward a friend who had deserted them." Defining capital as "the means of society," he offered the regulative principle that every man, according to his means, should be a producer; but he also asserted that "no man has absolute ownership," that "the state has rights of eminent domain," and that "society certainly has human rights." In the belief that "all men have reason to look for a Messiah for this life as well as for the life to come," Smyth suggested self-help, organization, and "increasing participation in common social interests" as possible paths to solution of the Social Question.[16]

Still other clergymen came to believe that the place of the Christian church was to stand unreservedly on the side of the laboring man. "The Church has a message to all men," declared one in 1887, but "we put the laborer first, because the Church is ever on the side of the weaker." A number of prominent clergymen stood firmly on the side of labor, as did many prominent Christian laymen. Among them were Charles Richmond Henderson, professor of sociology at the University of Chicago, and Richard T. Ely, professor of economics at the University of Wisconsin. At Yale University a group of undergraduates proposed a University Federation of Labor, through which students would have honorary memberships in local unions in New Haven, would write on labor themes for their degrees, would invite prominent labor leaders to give addresses, and would build a select labor library for the university.[17]

Without any doubt, however, the best and most extensive attempt of American Protestantism to bridge the gulf between churches and workingmen was the "institutional church" movement, which reached its climax in the 1890s. This "new religious movement" sought "to influence the whole life of the world, to lift up human society, to purify civic life, to make the city clean, politics honest and socially pure," in the belief that "the Church is not to be contented with hearing sermons; but it must practice what it hears, live what it believes."[18]

The institutional churches represented, perhaps, the work of influential laymen rather than the work of clergymen. In the 1880s various laymen had suggested that traditional forms of church culture did not interest the young; that the churches should provide "free places of worship, to be open at all hours," and that church life should be made "as alluring as the opera, the theatre, the lecture room, or even a political campaign meeting." The "aggressive missionary" work that they suggested—the method of "being all things to all men, in the apostle's meaning and not in the pulpit sensationalist's"— took shape in the institutional church movement.[19]

PEW RENTS

There was no American religious custom that offended workingmen, and the concerned Christian pastors and laymen who longed to reach out to them, more than the pew rental system. "The pew rental system belongs to a spirit and age of caste, thoroughly un-American," declared the Reverend Charles L. Thompson of New York City in 1896. A decade earlier, Professor Theodore W. Dwight, of Columbia College Law School, had written that the pew rental system did not exist in the early church, but had grown up in England "by special favor or . . . exclusiveness . . . contrary to the genuine spirit of Christianity."[20]

"I want to know what to do," implored a so-called typical churchgoer in 1878. "For more than a year have I tried to get reasonable accommodations for my family. I have tried to *hire* sittings enough. Our number is not very large; yet have they been divided around into three parts of the house, . . . dependent on the courtesy of friends. . . . I want my children to sit together; and two parents, if both are there, cannot sit in three places. . . . Is the church crowded? No. . . . Is the house small? No. . . . The trouble is, pews have been inherited. Owners will not part with them."[21]

"Pews have doors and locks," complained Richard T. Ely in 1886. "The aisles are guarded by ushers not merely to show people in, but to keep them out. Church privileges are sold. . . . It is monstrous to think of buying a favored place in God's house. . . . When the kingdom of heaven is put up at auction, of what can we think but the money-changers in the Temple at Jerusalem?"[22]

The American system of pew rentals was astonishingly complicated. It was a system of taxation "so adjusted that the well-to-do may furnish by far the larger part of the required income, . . . in close analogy with an income tax, with a property tax, and with custom duties by the State." The tax was thus fairly distributed, at least approximately, according to the capacity to pay. In some churches the pews were owned by individuals and were taxed from ten percent to twenty-five percent of their valuation. Some people owned several pews. In some churches the pews were owned by "the Society" and rented.[23]

The sale of church pews was also surprisingly lucrative. For example, when "the vendue" of the pews and benches occurred in November 1871 at Hopewell Reformed Church, "230 seats were sold to 157 different persons, some of them taking a whole bench of eight seats. The revenues from this sale more than paid for the cost of construction of the entire church."[24]

As Howard A. Bridgman noted in 1890, "The American atmosphere vibrates quickly and long whenever a note of freedom is struck. We . . . have a free government, a free press and free schools. . . . Our boast is of a gospel that . . . makes men free. . . . How easy, then, to argue onward to free churches and free pews."[25] This American spirit of freedom responded quickly and spontaneously to the cautious talk of "free pews" that began to circulate in Protestant churches in the 1870s, as was dramatically evidenced in the remarkable saga of the People's Church of Boston, the culmination of the dream of a Methodist pastor by the name of John William Hamilton for "a large Tabernacle church for the masses without class distinction."[26]

Appointed in 1872 to "the union of the Cockerel church on Hanover Street, and the Grace church on Temple Street, Boston," Hamilton entered vigorously upon a strong effort to buy Music Hall "for the Methodist denomination in general, and for these united congregations in particular." Cyrus Wakefield, at the head of the great rattan industry of the country, promised to give one-third of the purchase price of Music Hall, which was valued at three hundred thousand dollars. Wakefield, however, died unexpectedly before any legal securities had been given. Hamilton, nevertheless, did not give up his dream. He secured a very valuable lot of land and devised many ingenious methods of raising the needed money:

> One of the novel plans was the miniature representation of a brick lithographed on a card, on which was inscribed the words, 'The owner of this card has purchased one brick in the People's Church.' . . . Then the text, 'The rich and poor meet together; the Lord is the maker of them all.'

. . . Canvassing agents were employed and remunerated with a dollar's worth of books for every dollar's worth of cards sold. . . . Even feeble and invalid women . . . became devoted helpers in the work. . . . Miniature bricks were also made and sold as souvenirs; also little pots or bean jugs, with orifices for pennies were sent around. An elaborate autograph album was likewise made the means of collecting many a mite.[27]

In these unique ways, more than a hundred thousand people took part financially in building the People's Church. The opening services were held in February 1884, with "three monster meetings—morning, afternoon, and evening." The audience room was a model of comfort and convenience, the house beautifully lighted with porcelain reflectors, and the seats "in the form of an opera chair, but made of cherry and fitted with an ingenious hat-rack."[28]

In spite of such a spontaneous response, however, the idea of a free and open church was slow to gain acceptance. Many church members had deep reservations about the idea. Fears were expressed that free gifts would not pay the bills, that charities would not be provided for, that people were "not yet sanctified enough" for the free seat system, that the frequent change of members from one pew to another would dissipate the "home feeling" of regular attendants, and even that free pews would separate families and destroy family life.[29]

EPISCOPALIAN FREE CHURCHES

Many noted Social Gospelers took a direct part in the establishment of the People's Church, including Phillips Brooks, Edward Everett Hale, and Joseph Cook.[30] The credit, however, for the real beginnings of the free church in America must go to the Protestant Episcopal church, and especially to its vigorous Church Congress, "the significant voice of the people of this church that her mission was to be the American Church of the American people."[31]

A number of writers have emphasized the place of leadership held by the Episcopal church in efforts to provide a Christian ministry to labor, and in Protestant philanthropy in the nineteenth century.

Frederic Palmer, writing in the *Andover Review* in 1892, attributed this leadership to the fact that the Episcopalian ideas of the immanence of God and the solidarity of man were consonant with the philosophical thought and the secular trends of the nineteenth century, an age that increasingly emphasized democracy, organization, and the organic relations of life. While the Puritan Separatists had insisted that the true church must keep itself apart from the world, and the Presbyterians stressed the vital connection of man with man only on the side of sin and evil, the Church of England and its American counterpart taught, and reflected in their worship and usages, the belief that men are bound together by virtue of their common humanity, and that the church is "an institution which recognizes the world at large as in some true sense already God's, and does not confine this kinship to a select body taken out of the world. . . .

"The recognition of infants as members of the church equally with adults; the specialization of the different departments of ministerial work, each requiring specialists; . . . the congregation's active participation in worship . . . are all developments of the thought that man's relations are inherent and organic, whether these relations are to other men, to the kingdom of heaven, to the church, or to public worship."[32]

Thus, in the nineteenth century, the Episcopalian church was "a receptive and creative organism'' that was able to restore to American Protestantism Calvin's conception of the church as "a universal body, comprising all races, all classes, all types, and bound in one by internal bonds"—not by emphasizing Calvin's negative doctrine of predestination, but rather his doctrine of justification—that all of society should show forth the glory of God.[33]

The Protestant Episcopal Church Congress in America was the culmination of the celebrated Memorial Movement of the Convention of 1856. In England there was a parallel Church Congress, first begun in 1861 at Oxford University, which "helped to awaken a dormant Church to her duty to neglected masses, and . . . brought men of all schools of thought nearer together for common work." The American Congress was an indigenous effort "to plant the apostolic faith in this 'vast commonwealth of sects,' . . . to collect the general mind of the Church, to bring the best knowledge of the best men in the field to bear upon questions of the day."[34]

The Church Congress served as an educator of Christian lay opinion until well into the twentieth century. Even the first Congress, meeting in New York under very grave difficulties, exerted a marked influence upon public opinion. The papers read were "honest statements" published "in full in the great dailies." Men who had never seen a hymn-book or heard a church service "read them eagerly," for they "told men everywhere that the Episcopal Church is alive, and that her members have vital interests in common with all Christians."[35]

The second annual meeting of the Church Congress, held in Philadelphia in November 1875, discussed the subject of free churches and expressed a manifest desire to look about for new ways of work. It was reported that "every allusion to 'free churches' and 'free preaching' was applauded. . . . Many seemed to believe that Free Churches, meaning thereby, Churches without pew rents, would constitute the panacea for all the ills to which we are subject."[36]

By 1875 the Protestant Episcopal church in America already had a remarkable history of experience with free churches, beginning in 1846 with the Church of the Holy Communion, at the corner of Sixth Avenue and West Twentieth Street in New York City, reported to be the first free church in America and the first to be opened for daily services. Founded by the "sainted" William A. Muhlenberg, this church established the first "fresh air" work in the city of New York, the first employment society for poor women, and the first Anglican sisterhood in America. The establishment of a free dispensary led eventually to St. Luke's Hospital and St. Johnland's, a Christian community and home. Muhlenberg was succeeded by the Reverend Henry Mottet; and in 1885 there were nine hundred communicants on the church roll, supporting a baby shelter, an industrial school, a workingman's club, a relief association and literary club, a home for aged women, a shelter for respectable girls, a summer home at Hastings-on-the-Hudson, and a coal fund.[37]

In 1875 the Free and Open Church Association of the Protestant Episcopal church was founded. It advocated free churches "where no seats are appropriated, when all stand on an equal footing," each giving "through the offertory freely, and according to his means, to the support and work of the Church [and] works of benevolence and mercy." Among significant organizations fostered by this Association were the Church Association for the Advancement of the Interests of Labor (CAIL) and the Christian Social Union in America and Canada, which studied assiduously the works of Richard T. Ely, reportedly a staunch "Churchman" (Episcopalian layman) who had "the Christian enthusiasm of humanity which is always contagious among the ingenuous youth of our universities."[38]

By 1889 more than half of the Episcopalian churches in New York City were free. By 1898 more than eighty-two percent of the Episcopalian churches in America were free, with "over two hundred churches . . . open daily for private prayer and meditation."[39] Two of the most famous were St. George's and St. Bartholomew's in New York, considered by many to be the most representative institutional churches in America. Two of the most unusual were the Galilee Mission of Calvary Parish and the Church of the Transfiguration, also both in New York.

Although not a free church, the Galilee Mission featured "co-operative methods" to support enterprises on behalf of men and boys on the East Side to whom city life had brought "privation and poverty, temptation and disaster." Its rector was the Reverend Henry G. Satterlee, later called to be bishop of Washington. Its unique activities included the Olive Tree Inn and Restaurant, both self-supporting. The price of a night's lodging was from fifteen to twenty-five cents. Over three hundred persons could be accommodated, and more than a hundred thousand lodgings were sold in one year. There was also a woodyard and a successful boys' club of over four hundred members.[40]

The Church of the Transfiguration, situated on Twenty-ninth Street between the old "Tenderloin" and the city morgue, had only two rectors in the first seventy-five years of its history: the founder, George Hendric Houghton, who died in 1897 after a ministry of half a century and was succeeded by his nephew, George Clarke Houghton. The elder Houghton was "among the first in America" to join the movement for the Catholic revival in the Angelican communion spearheaded in England by John Keble, the famous Oxford divine and poet. Houghton also became the controversial national spiritual father of actors and actresses, whom he called "the kindly folk." The younger Houghton began his pastoral career in Hoboken, where he was the pioneer of "self-helpful works . . . which help the poor by teaching them how to help themselves." He also served as superintendent of public instruction in Hudson County, New Jersey, and as president of the Industrial Education Association of New Jersey. Both men were "militant believers in all the ancient forms of their Church"; but they were also men who "put humanity ahead of theology," knowing that, to the needy, food and clothes and a job were "more urgent than prayer."

George Hendric Houghton had begun his ministry under William A. Muhlenberg as curate at the Church of the Holy Communion. There he administered the sacraments to blacks and to the destitute at Bellevue Hospital, as well as to "a multitude of Medes, Parthians, and dwellers in the V Avenue" at the usual "fancy service." His experiences in "the gaunt wards of hospital and asylum" led him to "a new dream—a parish among the poor."

In 1848 he began services for six communicants and a transient group of forty or fifty people, in the rear room of a home on Twenty-fourth Street. By 1850 there were forty communicants, who built an "unpretentious" one-story building on Twenty-ninth Street, "in the midst of vacant lots, . . . back from the street." By 1864 "the modest temple . . . had grown, addition by addition, to a church with a seating capacity of over one thousand"; yet the building had "a simple dignity touched by quaintness," with free pews for "less favored brethren" and, outside, "little houses for the birds."

In the 1860s, with the appearance of the "elegant brownstone fronts" of Fifth Avenue, Houghton's church became a rich man's congregation largely made up of the fashionable elite; yet it offered refuge to large numbers of blacks on the underground route to Canada, and the church's most-used appliances were Houghton's night bell and speaking tube, which summoned him at any hour to minister to the dying in the resorts of the old Tenderloin, then at its most lurid period.

In 1870 the Church of the Transfiguration achieved sudden national fame as "a little church around the corner" that offered to provide a Christian funeral for the popular comic actor George Holland after he had been refused burial by William T. Sabine, the rector of the Church of the Atonement. The popularity of Holland, and also "the fact that the refusal of the rites of Christian burial had come at the Christmas season," caused a national wave of "indignant protest," with testimonial demonstrations at theaters and opera houses throughout the country. Houghton's church became known far and wide as the Little Church Around the Corner—the subject of poems, a hit minstrel song, and later a successful New York play, a novel, and a movie. Houghton's name became a household word synonymous with "a broad and tolerant charity." His church was granted an unprecedented "grand testimonial" by the drama and minstrel profession of "breezy, big-hearted Chicago"; actors and actresses forwarded their gifts to Houghton's church, where a charity fund was established to aid "impoverished parishes" in various states of the Union, as well as "famine-stricken multitudes in France," and victims of the Chicago fire of 1871. Houghton's courageous ministry to the theatrical profession also led to founding the Actors Church Alliance at All Souls Church in Chicago. The Alliance was founded by "a Reverend Bentley of theatrical background," and had "nearly a thousand members . . . in almost all the States" by 1901.[41]

St. George's, a rich church spending over a hundred thousand dollars annually, with an endowment fund, begun in 1891, of twice that amount, was also a "frontier" church, facing that "pitiful wilderness of human life below 14th Street," a "notable instance of the institutional church which does its work not by proxy and at long range, but at first hand and within its own precincts."[42]

The rector of St. George's, William S. Rainsford, was possibly the most widely known, and certainly one of the most active and controversial institutional church clergymen. His church also employed four assistants and four deaconesses, besides specialists in charge of the athletic and industrial departments. Boasting a five-floor building with someone on duty "all the time," St. George's had, among other things, physicians in attendance one hour each morning, an industrial school, a relief department, a grocery and clothes room, a periodical club, chapters of the King's Daughters and the Boys' Brigade—and, last but far from least, its famous cottage for mothers and children by the sea at Rockaway Park. This immense and varied parish work was all based on the idea that "you cannot sow any seeds of religious truth in the hearts of poor people," except in connection with entertainment and recreation that will win their trust and confidence. "Give them such fun," concluded the members of St. George's, "and their natures slowly unbend, they mix with each other, and . . . they are ripe for the light of the Gospel."[43]

St. Bartholomew's, said to be the richest parish in America, boasted the finest parish house in the city of New York. Cornelius Vanderbilt donated the lot. His mother, Mrs. William H. Vanderbilt, erected and furnished the building at a total cost of four hundred thousand dollars. The architects were instructed to have "nothing ecclesiastical about the architecture, the idea . . . being that it should be devoted to humanitarian as well as religious objects." The basement floor of the parish house included a handsome luncheon room on the plan of an English coffee house, a lavatory where poor women could do their washing, and a complete kindergarten, "conducted according to the most advanced methods." Other floors contained a cooking school, an industrial school, and a gymnasium. The parish house was under the special charge of the Reverend C.A. Carsten, a Dane by birth, and formerly general missioner of the Episcopal Parochial Missions Society.

The motto of the church was that worship is "hard work, and cannot be of much service . . . unless engaged in"; that "every pew should be a missionary pew, and every regular occupant . . . a missionary." The church conducted Swedish, Turkish, Armenian, Syrian, Chinese, and other missions and Sunday schools. Its expenditures amounted to more than $150,000 annually; and the minister, the Reverend David H. Greer, had five assistants, twenty lay readers, and a group of parish visitors.

In 1895 St. Bartholomew's opened its famous loan association, a pawn shop to lend money on household goods and chattel mortgage at the legal six percent rate of interest. This idea was copied in Chicago, St. Louis, Minneapolis, and other cities. Later the church opened a clinic and a large rescue mission work, with its Rescue Mission Workers' Practical Training School, under the leadership of Colonel H.H. Hadley.[44]

BERKELEY TEMPLE

All of this vigorous work of the Episcopalian Church came, significantly, to the attention of William Jewett Tucker, president of Dartmouth College. "The Episcopal Church," he wrote in 1885, "is growing in numbers and influence. . . . If it is to become, as some predict, the church of the city, it will not be because of its social position, or from the attractions of the liturgy, or for the freedom of its faith, but because it is organizing itself more thoroughly, studying more carefully the use of its means, and providing a more abundant ministry than any other Protestant denomination."[45]

Tucker was deeply concerned about the problems of city churches and fired with a Christian commitment to achieve, in whatever ways humanly possible, the evangelization of American cities. He admitted that the methods of the chapel, as "an appendage of a distant and wealthy church," and the city mission, working through "small and unfurnished stations," had previously been "most satisfactory to the Church and to the city." He also noted, however, that "the city is fast developing a population that falls between the church and the chapel" and became convinced that city evangelization would not be accomplished until "the church of the city" equipped itself for work "every day in the week," ministering through "all possible agencies" and penetrating into "the densest life of the city."[46]

Tucker believed that the Congregationalists could learn much from the Episcopalians and was no doubt instrumental in bringing Episcopalian free church methods to Berkeley Temple in Boston, where the Reverend Charles A. Dickinson became pastor in 1888. Berkely Temple was the first church in America to be called "institutional." It was also called the "Church of Young America" and described as a duplication of Tolman's Square Congregational Church in London.[47] It stood "at the intersection of avenues, one of which leads immediately to the homes of wealth, . . . another of which opens right upon scenes of vice and misery, and still another is connected with the dwelling-places of that immense class of people who . . . go their own way." The surrounding boarding and lodging houses, "with Legion for their name," harbored a mighty army of young men and women "adrift from the restraining influences of home." Boys and girls by the thousands, to whom home was merely a place for eating and sleeping, swarmed in the city streets, "learning Satan's lessons at an age and with a facility that would shock anyone who could know in detail the dreadful facts of the case."[48]

The Berkeley Temple "experiment" began with Dickinson, two assistant pastors, and several lay workers. The church's basic purpose was ministry, and it welcomed "anything that would help reach the people," noting that some needed shoes, some were hungry and others were sick, all needed "counsel, sympathy, and instruction," and all "needed supremely" the "satisfying Gospel of Jesus Christ."

The Berkeley Temple ministry included a relief department, an employment bureau, medical and legal bureaus, and a boarding house register, all free. Three hundred women were enrolled in evening classes in dressmaking, stenography, millinery, painting, elocution, and languages. The Young Men's Institute included a reading room, a modest gymnasium, a literary club, Tuesday evening entertainments, and a public ice-water fountain in front of the church, "a potent factor for temperance in the neighborhood." In fact, Berkeley Temple was constantly at work in behalf of temperance. For a time it operated a temperance rescue and gold-cure establishment in Vermont, featuring the "Thompson cure." This was later converted into a home for boys "where forty little wanderers from the street of the city find shelter, education and *home*." There was also, on a smaller scale, a home for girls.

From at least 1892, Berkeley Temple sponsored the Andover Band, which provided field work for students at Andover seminary. In the autumn of 1894 the Temple opened a School of Applied Christianity, with the Reverend Lawrence Phelps as principal. All of the students "at once" became part of the active work force of the church. It was reported that "they find out the needs of the people, come directly in contact with them, and are taught how to carry on this work of evangelization." The Newspaper Class, begun in October 1891, provided informal discussions on current events and movements, with its members taking note of Congressional proceedings and reporting on measures of importance. The church newspaper was the *Berkeley Beacon,* which was "much more free than some papers of its class from a certain sanctimonious 'goody-goody' flavor."

All in all, Berkeley Temple was a remarkable "religious family on a larger scale" with "a great abounding religious life," including twelve distinct services on Sunday, seven prayer meetings each week, and Sunday schools for Chinese, Armenians, and Greeks. In myriad and spectacular ways the Temple carried out its stated objectives of "evangelization, Christian nurture of the young, and practical Christian work."[49]

The name "institutional church"—first applied to Berkeley Temple—is credited to Tucker, who asked in 1886: "Why should not a great church in a great city be an institution? Why should not its doors be open every day of the week, with services upon each day fitted to the religious wants of the people within its reach?"[50] The name was considered cumbersome by its very users and was certainly misleading; for "religion as a life, and not the church as an institution" was the essential aim of the whole movement, which sought "to escape out of the old life of the church as an institution into the free air of the world." This new conception of the mission of a church found expression "in word and work" in many places, but "it awaited crystalization into such definite shape that it could appeal to the world at large. It needed a name and a definition." These it found in Berkeley Temple.[51]

THE OPEN AND INSTITUTIONAL CHURCH LEAGUE

Two of the clearest spokesmen for the institutional church movement were the well-known Methodist clergyman Harry F. Ward and the Reverend Charles S. Mills of the Pilgrim Congregational Church in Cleveland, and later of North Brookfield, Massachusetts. Both of them emphasized the inductive development of the underlying principles and ideals of the movement. Mills said in 1892 that "the perfect form is yet to come," and Ward wrote in 1900 that the institutional church was "born of the storm and stress of actual conflict with . . . harsh realities."[52]

In the 1890s, however, prominent institutional church pastors began to deduce descriptive definitions of the type of church they were working with. The Reverend John L. Scudder, pastor of the Jersey City Tabernacle defined it thus:

> The Institutional Church is one that ministers to the varied wants of man, and not to the spiritual element alone. Such wants are physical, industrial, social, mental, educational, aesthetic. It proceeds upon the principle that anything secular but sinless is religious, and uses anything that will lift men up to a better life, and shield them from temptation.[53]

The most widely quoted definition was that of the Reverend Edward Judson of New York:

> An Institutional Church, then, is an organized body of Christian believers, who, finding themselves in a hard and uncongenial social environment, supplement the ordinary methods of the Gospel . . . by a system of organized kindness, a congeries of institutions, which, by touching people on physical, social, and intellectual sides, will conciliate them and draw them within reach of the Gospel.[54]

"The Institutional Church no longer aims to save the man by sections, it aims to save the whole man . . . because all of him needs saving," wrote Ward, who then continued:

> The Institutional Church presents a complete organism. . . . The Church also recognizes that this individual organism is one of the members of the great social organism. . . . He cannot be saved out of the body politic; it must be saved with him. So that the aim of this movement becomes also the salvation of the family, of the community, of the great social order.[55]

In the spring of 1894 a group of institutional church pastors organized the Open and Institutional Church League in New York City. It represented "about forty churches in different part of the country." The platform of the League, the "first deliberate expression" of the aim of the institutional church, read as follows:

> The open and institutional church depends upon the development of a certain spirit, rather than upon the aggregation of special appliances and methods.
>
> Inasmuch as the Christ came not to be ministered unto, but to minister, the open and institutional church, filled and moved by His spirit of ministering love, seeks to become the center and source of all beneficent and philanthropic effort, and to take the leading part in every movement which has for its end the alleviation of human suffering, the elevation of man, and the betterment of the world.
>
> Thus the open and institutional church aims to save all men and all of the man by all means, abolishing so far as possible the distinction between the religious and secular, and sanctifying all days and all means to the great end of saving the world for Christ.
>
> While the open and institutional church is known by its spirit of ministration rather than by any specific methods of expressing that spirit, it stands for open church doors for every day and all the day, free seats, a plurality of

Christian workers, the personal activity of all church members, a ministry to all the community through educational, reformatory, and philanthropic channels, to the end that men may be won to Christ and His service, that the church may be brought back to the simplicity and comprehensiveness of its primitive life, until it can be said of every community, 'The Kingdom of Heaven is within you' and 'Christ is all in all.'[56]

URBAN INSTITUTIONAL CHURCHES

Institutional churches began, typically, in downtown churches, in old plants not well adapted. Such was the case with Bethany Presbyterian Church, Philadelphia; Cornell Memorial Church, New York; Asbury Methodist Church, New York; and Morgan Chapel, Boston. Bethany was headed by the Reverend J. Wilbur Chapman, "reputed to rank with Mr. Moody among the foremost evangelists" of the time. Its Bethany Bible Union, with a recorded attendance of 2,550 on one occasion, carried on systematic visitation by "tithemen" and women, each of whom was given the oversight of ten members. It had a separate building for its Sunday School of three thousand people, and an entire building of forty rooms for its famous Bethany College, of which John Wanamaker was president and the Reverend Charles A. Dickey, director. "What people wish to know, Bethany College is willing to teach" was the boast of this evening school, with pupils ranging in age from twelve to forty years of age. The cost of tuition for the entire winter term was one to two dollars, and more than fifty scholarships were to open to competition.[57]

Cornell Memorial Methodist Episcopal Church stood midway between Fifth Avenue and the East River in New York City, in easy touch with fifty thousand people of all nationalities. "A true mediator between the rich and the poor, knowing no preferences, a friend to both," it had a kindergarten, a kitchen-garden, an athletic club, and an orchestra of twelve pieces that gave concerts and entertainments free of charge.

Cornell Memorial was moved to ask, "What is life worth here on the East Side? When sickness comes, the poor are hurried like cattle to our hospitals, and very quickly the story of another life is over, and there is another grave in Potter's field. Pinched, hungry faces one may see every day. . . . There are many families where self-support . . . seems to be an impossibility. . . .

"In this maelstrom of humanity, . . . the church must come as a practically free institution, at least in its first approach to the poor. Often the very first contact must be that of the Good Samaritan, relieving the suffering, caring for the dying, and paying the bills they cannot pay. . . . Our very success among these people is our embarrassment."[58]

Morgan Chapel in Boston, with the Reverend E.J. Helms as pastor, was famous for its free Saturday night concerts. It was reported that "an excellent musical and literary program," beginning at eight o'clock, was followed by "a rousing temperance meeting . . . held until eleven o'clock, when the saloons close. At last a cup of strong coffee is given to those who desire it, and under its counteracting influence many a man has gone home sober. Thousands have signed the pledge and foresworn an intemperate life."

The Chapel also carried on a trade school providing self-help for printers thrown out of work by the typesetting machines, destitute cobblers and carpenters, and hundreds of poor people sent by associated charities and other organizations. "Approved" women repaired partly-worn garments one afternoon each week for ten cents an hour. Applicants were investigated, if possible, and given work appropriate to their need and ability. Some work was pieced out to the homes of applicants.[59]

The Reverend James S. Stone came to Asbury Methodist Church, on the east side of Washington Square, New York, after working among the Eurasians in Bombay, India. Aiming to reach the poorer people among the wage-earning class, he first held religious services every Sunday evening, at which each attendant was given a sandwich and a cup of coffee; but he concluded that the experiment was not a success, for "the people entered with great spirit into the edible part of the meeting, but took a very languid interest in the services at the close. The worst feature . . . was that it kept away from the church . . . the very people it sought especially to reach."

Stone, therefore, turned to other methods, such as "a pleasant hour for workingmen and their wives" every Sunday evening at half-past six. The first half-hour was devoted to a sacred concert, the last half to an address. Each member paid two cents a week. Books were given as prizes for regular attendance. Stone also opened a woodyard, a dispensary, a kindergarten, and carried on street preaching in the summer. A physician as well as a clergyman, he believed in "the Keeley and the Morrell cures for drunkenness." One of his dreams was to start "a saloon without any liquor, . . . elegantly fitted up, with beautiful mirrors, and bright with electric lights." With the coming of the Reverend W. F. Anderson, Asbury Church entered a new epoch. The parsonage was reconstructed as a parish house with a day nursery, clubs for the young people, and a gymnasium in the basement.[60]

Some institutional churches, such as First Baptist, Philadelphia, had rented pews. At First Baptist the pew rents yielded about ten thousand dollars yearly, but at the beginning of each service all seats were free. A church rule required, however, that every person must contribute at least one cent a year. It was reported that "those who are so poor that they cannot give, not only receive sittings, but are helped in paying their rent."

The Reverend George Dana Boardman served this parish from 1864 to 1894, when the Reverend Kerr Boyce Tupper was called from Denver, Colorado. He divided the city into twelve districts, placing over each, as supervisor, a deacon. Among the clubs carried on by the chuch were a Girls' Guild and a Boys' Brigade "with military drill and real guns."[61]

Other institutional churches, however, such as Holland Memorial Presbyterian Church of Philadelphia, were "born free." Holland raised seventy-five thousand dollars a year through an "envelope" system, with each contributor giving "as the Lord has prospered him." The pastors were the Reverend William M. Paden and the Reverend J.R. Miller. Besides numerous clubs, a building and loan association, and a beneficial organization guaranteeing to its members "five dollars a week for ten weeks in case of illness, and fifty dollars in case of death," the congregation had a thriving university extension relationship with the YMCA and broadened its own library into "a branch of the Free Library in the City of Philadelphia to be located in the YMCA rooms."[62]

In 1897 the president of the Open and Institutional Church League was the Reverend Charles L. Thompson, pastor of the Madison Avenue Presbyterian Church, a prominent church which adopted the free church principle as a sharp reversal of policy. In 1891 the church was thinking of selling its building, but it abruptly chose an alternate course: that it "should follow . . . the example of St. George's and St. Bartholomew's . . . and . . . become positively and aggressively a people's church." The entire required sum of fifteen thousand dollars was then subscribed within ten minutes. This new departure proved to be successful; the institutional features of the church's work included clubs for girls and boys, a kindergarten, a "penny provident" fund, a library, and a "helping hand" society.[63]

Another famous church which became institutional deliberately was the Fourth Con-grergrational Church of Hartford, Connecticut. Founded in 1832, it had reached the point where "it had to readjust or die." Then in 1880 Graham Taylor was called to the pastorate. "In his mind were already stirring the ideas respecting the application of Christianity through the church to the whole life of man." In 1892 a group of laymen petitioned Taylor to establish an institutional church, in the belief that such a church "is necessary in the development of truer Christian character, purer and more noble manhood, . . . better Christians and better citizens, in city, in state, and in nation."[64]

One interesting feature of Fourth Church was its chapter of the Christian Industrial League, which was founded in 1893 at Hope Church, Springfield, Massachusetts, by the Reverend David Allen Reed, president of the Normal Bible College (formerly the School of Christian Workers), "to provide an organization in the churches which would bring men into touch with the churches, and which would afford every social and benevolent advantage which any similar order can furnish outside the churches." At Fourth Church, in return for an admission fee of fifty cents and monthly dues of forty cents, a sickness benefit of four dollars a week was paid for thirteen weeks, and then two dollars per week for thirteen weeks additional, if necessary, with the services of a chapter physician furnished free of charge.[65]

Some churches, such as Beacon Presbyterian, in the manufacturing district of Kensington, Philadelphia, were set up from the beginning as institutional churches. Beacon was inaugurated in 1885 under the leadership of the Reverend Francis L. Robbins and the Reverend James M. Marr. The Reverend Wellington E. Loucke was called to the church in March 1894. The Beacon buildings, built with contributions from "influential firms and individuals," contained the offices of the "Northeast Society for Organizing Charity, covering five wards of the city"; a funeral vault, "cemented, dry and clean," to "mitigate" the expenses of burial; a dispensary where nine physicians daily contributed their services, charging a small fee and thus "preventing pauperization"; and Beacon College, founded "to supply the needs of multitudes who have passed the school age, and find their lives hampered by ignorance [but] will not go to a city night school."[66]

There were also a few colorful congregations that had their institutional beginnings in the heat of the abolition movement or in activities connected with the Civil War. The most famous of these was Tremont Temple in Boston, with its annual newsboys' and bootblacks' Thanksgiving, dating from 1877; its Bible classes, maintaining "a perfect social organization, caring for the invalid, the poor, or unfortunate"; and its large number of conversions resulting from Sunday school work with youth who were strangers to the city.

Tremont Temple was founded by Timothy Gilbert, "wealthy piano manufacturer, devout Baptist, and 'hot-headed Abolitionist,'" who, in 1840, vowing that "there shall be a church in this haughty city, Boston, where a fugitive slave can sit beside me to worship our Father," purchased the Tremont Theater, where Wendell Phillips had "rocked the cradle of emancipation," Sumner had "roused the populace," and Everett had spoken so often "that it became almost his pulpit."

The Temple was destroyed by fire in 1852 and again in 1879. In 1880 the rebuilt church merged with the Merrimac Street Baptist Church to become the Union Temple Baptist Church. It boasted five pastors, two deaconesses, and an average Sunday attendance of ten thousand; it claimed that in the fifty years of its history more than twenty million persons had assembled on that plot of ground "for religious, political, and esthetic social purposes." From the beginning, Gilbert had dubbed his church "a Stranger's Sabbath

Home"; and early every Sunday morning a large committee of young men went to railway stations, to hotels, and to boarding houses, "bearing invitations from the Stranger's Church."

Tremont Temple sought to avoid the "ecclesiastical dread" that prevented many from "venturing into stately Gothic aisles," and advertised itself as offering "not 'sensationalism,' not politics, not disputed social problems, but the religion of the soul." It rented the street floor of its building and its large halls for "every denominational gathering of a general character" and for "the most brilliant literary and musical events of Boston winter life." Its building also housed the *Watchman* (the Baptist newspaper of New England), the Social Union, and the headquarters of various Protestant denominations.[67]

Dickinson classified the secular work of institutional churches under three heads: relief, entertainment, and instruction. Ward made essentially the same classificiation, into "educational, social recreational, and charitable." Russell H. Conwell, the Baptist preacher of *Acres of Diamonds* fame, divided institutional work into "the three kinds of work in which Christ labored: viz., teaching the ignorant, healing the sick, and preaching the Gospel."[68]

Berkeley Temple was representative of those churches that concentrated on education. Asbury Methodist was typical of those emphasizing charitable works and preaching. When it came to sheer entertainment, however, the Jersey City Tabernacle with its People's Palace had no peer. The institutional work of the Tabernacle was begun by the Reverend A.P. Foster in 1878. By 1890 the church was under the leadership of the Reverend John L. Scudder and his wife, "doing a missionary work worthy of their missionary name."[69]

Jersey City never had "a remarkably savory reputation," and its municipal government was notoriously corrupt. Scudder concluded that "only as his church should strike out new lines could it make any impression on the mass of humanity close to its very doors." He borrowed some of his ideas from the Reverend J. Lester Wells in Newark. In due time Wells became an assistant to Scudder. The Tabernacle carried out the ordinary purposes of a church; the People's Palace, "on the lines of the famous London institution," became its unique annex, lying near "the sharp line of demarcation which in that part of Jersey City severs a region of residences from the crowded tenement district."

It was claimed that the People's Palace of Jersey City "gives all that the saloon gives, minus the liquor, and charges less." It had a capacious amusement hall in which ten-pins cost only five cents per man; billiards twenty cents an hour; pool three cents a cue or two cues for five cents; shuffle-board a nickle apiece; and bagatelle, crokinole, quoits, and thirty different kinds of small games, "absolutely free." The Palace was not self-supporting, "although it was not in debt." The work was carried on "in a manly and healthy fashion and in a genuinely Christian spirit." The activities of the church included a library, a reading room, debating societies, Chautauquan circles; a gymnasium, a swimming tank, and outdoor grounds for tennis and military drill; a day nursery, clothiery, and classes in sewing, dressmaking, typesetting, drawing, and singing; and an employment bureau, a boarding house bureau, and "various societies."[70]

Institutional churches, typically, worked with thoroughness of organization and division of labor of an extent that "would gratify a pronounced bureaucrat." One of the editors of *Open Church,* the official organ of the Open and Institutional Church League, wrote in 1897: "Order is Heaven's first law. When God works either in nature or in grace, His work is methodical and orderly, and if man is to be a successful co-worker with God, his work must also be characterized by system and method."[71]

The larger institutional churches were certainly a product of an age of organization, an age in which corporations were "the favorite method employed."[72] Business methods prevailed at Berkeley Temple and the Jersey City Tabernacle, but Ruggles Street Baptist Church in Boston was a veritable model of business efficiency and orderly system. This "vigorous, pulsating, evangelical church" was presided over by the Reverend Everett D. Burr, prominent in "all civic movements that make for truth and righteousness." Burr described his church as having "utter simplicity of organization," with a "minimum of politics and a maximum of power."

Burr's church worked in "constant cooperation and sympathy with the Associated Charities." At the base of the church's operations was the visitor. Every family in the district was visited at least twice a year. In 1897 the church reported that it gave away 25,956 pounds of food, 36 tons of coal, 29 pieces of furniture, and $7,957.48 in money; but no gifts were bestowed "until after the most painstaking investigation." Besides the relief department, there was a dispensary and a maternity department, which offered "a constant course of instruction in hygiene and household economics." The church also maintained an apparatus for sterilizing milk and supplied a daily average of twenty-nine babies and four mothers in 1897. Believing that "youth of American birth . . . are the most serious sufferers from the lack of manual training," the church carried on Friendford Industrial School, where "whatever is needed is taught."[73]

Ruggles Street was one of five Baptist institutional churches in Boston, all of which had free seats. There were three more in New York: Mount Morris Baptist Church, Harlem, "the first church in New York City to advertise classes in eugenics"; Amity Baptist Church, led by the Reverend Leighton Williams, the son of an "honored father," with "scanty resources and large ideals, . . . broad sympathies and . . . intense moral earnestness"; and Judson Memorial Baptist Church, built in honor of the first American foreign missionary, Adoniram Judson, who introduced Christianity into Burma.[74]

His son, the Reverend Edward Judson, chose the site for the Judson Memorial "with much deliberation and great sagacity." He believed that it should be "in lower New York . . . on the borderland between the rich and the poor," and that "the seats should be perpetually free." The cost of the location was $111,000; and the completed building cost $128,000 raised by "a myriad of contributions ranging from ten cents up." On the western section of the property was "The Judson," an apartment house built in architectural harmony with the church, and yielding an endowment income of $10,000 a year for the manifold educational, missionary, and philanthropic work of the church.[75]

The paragon of Baptist institutional churches was, of course, Grace Baptist in Philadelphia, more widely known as "Conwell's Temple," after its pastor, Russell H. Conwell. The Temple was reportedly the largest Protestant congregation in the United States, with membership of about two thousand, a paid staff of over one hundred, a recorded maximum attendance of over six thousand; and the "largest church auditorium for a Protestant congregation in America," seating some four thousand people. If the exterior suggested an art museum or library, the interior reminded one of a hotel, with plush orchestra chairs, an enormous organ presided over by David Wood, the blind organist; and a chorus choir of perhaps 250 voices, "all required to be professing Christians." From the immense gallery behind the platform, a stream of water ran down in a kind of cascade to the baptismal pool.[76]

To the pastor, his church was obviously a second home. Of tall and athletic frame, of cheery manners, the Reverend Conwell, it was reported, "looks like what he is—the chief factor in this cluster of enterprises." The following description was typical:

He seems like a great dynamo, . . . bearing the unmistakable tokens of born leadership. . . . During the singing he seems to take the look of a precentor because he cannot help doing so. With hand or hymnbook he marks the time. . . . Upon his knees in prayer you seem to hear one of God's children, reading simply for the other children, to a Father who listens well pleased. . . .

The sermon . . . is full of the straight homely words of conversation. His illustrations are all alike, pictorial, flashed upon the audience, and then dropped. . . . The preacher talks as a brother man to brother man out of his own experience. . . .

After an evening service, we follow the preacher up a stairway . . . to . . . an after-meeting. . . . Dr. Conwell seats himself at the organ, and accompanied by a small orchestra, leads in the singing of gospel hymns.[77]

With admission to the Temple by ticket only, "Conwell's Temple" admirable fulfilled its pastor's definition of preaching, teaching, and healing, with its Sunday Breakfast Association; its Samaritan Hospital, established in 1892, with a training school for nurses; and its famous Temple College, with a student body limited to "employees," but "prepared to give the same course as Princeton, and to confer the same degrees."[78]

Perhaps the best known institutional church in the Midwest was Plymouth Congregational Church in Indianapolis, where Oscar C. McCulloch succeeded Henry Ward Beecher to the pastorate in 1877. Under the pastorship of McCulloch, Plymouth Church became widely known as the "House of Life" with the "open door." McCulloch turned his church into a people's college by founding the Plymouth Institute, which emphasized "systematic courses of reading and study in the works of Hawthorne, Emerson, Kingsley, Spencer, Froebel, Lowell, Tolstoi, Carlyle, Mazzini, and Ruskin." There were also classes in drawing, design, music, languages, and physical training; lectures, concerts, and exhibitions; a kindergarten, sewing and cooking classes, and "many forms of self-help."[79]

Other institutional churches in the Midwest included the Reverend Simon Gilbert's Plymouth Church in Minneapolis, dating back to 1857 and noted for its "thorough organization, benevolent responsiveness," and its Bethel in the Scandinavian Quarter; the Pilgrim Congregational Church in Cleveland, under the Reverend Charles S. Mills; the Reverend Goodell's Pilgrim Church in St. Louis, reportedly "never closed"; the People's Church, St. Paul, with its cooking school; Plymouth Church, Milwaukee; Plymouth Tabernacle, Institute, and People's College, Detroit; Lagonda Avenue Church, Springfield, Ohio; and Plymouth Church, Salina, Kansas.[80] There were also free pew churches in Florida, Wyoming, Arizona, Colorado, and California. As they migrated westward, Americans apparently tended to discard the pew rental system.[81]

In Chicago, it was reported, it could "hardly be said that the church people were building up institutional churches." The name was even "offensive in some places." Church leaders, however, were driven to seek new devices and to experiment, with varying success, as they pursued "the tremendous task of assimilating a constantly growing foreign element."[82]

One of the experiments that succeeded was Plymouth Congregational Church, under the leadership of the Reverend Frank W. Gunsaulus, "near the homes of wealthy people, but also not far from streets of modest dwellings," with "vast hotels" rising in the neighborhood to house the modern "cave dwellers." Closely associated with Plymouth Church enterprises were the celebrated Armour Mission and Armour Institute, the splendid outgrowth of a little Sunday school organized in June 1871. In 1881, Joseph F. Armour left a bequest of a hundred thousand dollars for "the care of children and youth" through "preventive measures, religious and educational." As a benevolent man, he had often found work with adult paupers and criminals very discouraging. Armour Institute was, in reality, a group of charities in the heart of a depraved district of the South Side, including an apartment house, a kindergarten, and a dispensary, all "handsomely endowed by the wealthy packer"—a policy that characterized Chicago charities in general. The Chicago Manual Training School, the Newsboys' Home, and the Home for Incurables were all so endowed.[83]

Another spectacular success in Chicago was All Souls Church, with its unique Unitarian pastor, Jenkin Lloyd Jones; its famous Browning Club, its early use of the university extension idea, and its emphasis on "interpretation of the great thinkers and leaders" of the nineteenth century, "that they might become real sources of spiritual . . . growth." This particular cultural emphasis blossomed into the Abraham Lincoln Center, which is still active in the twentieth century in one of the poorest parts of the city.[84]

The history of Grace Church of Chicago was "unique among the Church annals of Chicago, and, one might add, of the West." Its St. Luke's Hospital, with its 120 beds, its "perfectly appointed" ward for children, and its training school for nurses, was the fruit of efforts of a number of "noble women" who had banded themselves together as the Camp Douglas Aid Society to prepare bandages and other necessities for the soldiers stationed in their midst during the Civil War.[85]

Immanuel Baptist Church of Chicago was in the "black belt" of the South Side, where "the catholic and democratic feeling could not be put to a more severe test." It maintained a Boys' Brigade, a German prayer meeting, and an industrial school for girls on Saturday. The pastor, the Reverend Johnston Myers, reportedly "firmly held" to the doctrine of plurality of trained workers and was "strongly opposed to amateur visitors and helpers, except under the leadership of the competent."[86]

SUBURBAN, SMALL-TOWN, AND RURAL
INSTITUTIONAL CHURCHES

Institutional church leaders emphasized that the idea of a "free and open" church offered "distinct suggestions" to many rural churches and a "cosmopolitan" pattern that could be applied "anywhere." They noted that "the average of morality is no higher in the village than in the city," and that "the whole man needs attention in the village as much as anywhere else."[87]

Although most institutional churches sprang up or developed in metropolitan areas and larger cities, they were also found in smaller towns and rural areas. As early as 1872, Mark Twain described a new church building to be built by Thomas K. Beecher for his Congregational parish in Elmira, New York. "When a Beecher projects a church," remarked Mark Twain, "that edifice is necessarily going to be something entirely fresh and original; . . . as variegated, eccentric, and marked with as peculiar and striking an individualism as a Beecher himself."

The proposed new church described by Mark Twain was to have three buildings. The main building—the church proper—was to contain a circular auditorium, an amphitheater "after the ordinary pattern of an opera-house," seating a thousand persons, with pews in graduated tiers and seats on the level floor for the aged and infirmed. There was to be no steeple, since "no practical use can be made of it"; no bell, "because all men know what time church service begins without that exasperating nuisance," and no wasted space. Under the raised tiers of pews were to be "stalls for horses and carriages, . . . mailed with 'deadeners,' and so thoroughly plastered, that neither sound nor smell can ascend to the church and offend the worshippers." The outside base of the church would, consequently, have "a formidable port-holed look, like a man-of-war."

The second building was to be a two-storied Sunday school building, with the upper story to be a "well-lighted and ventilated" children's playroom, "open and welcome to them through all the weekdays, . . . furnished with dumbbells, swings, rocking-horses, . . . to make the child look upon a church as only another *home,* and a sunny one, rather than as a dismal exile or a prison."

The third building was to have three stories. The first floor would house the "church parlours," a reception room, a free circulating library, and six bathrooms, utilizing waste steam from the church buildings, with free tickets issued to "any applicant among the unclean of the congregation" not able to pay for baths at the town barber shops. The second floor would house the lodging rooms for the janitresses—" for they will be women, Mr. Beecher holding that women are tidier and more efficient"; the permanent residence of the "church missionary," a lady who "constantly looks after the poor and sick of the church"; and an infirmary of six rooms, with "one or two waterbeds . . . and half-a-dozen reclining invalid-chairs on wheels." The third story of the building would house the church kitchen, "sensibly placed aloft, so that the ascending noises and boarding-house smells shall go up and aggravate the birds instead of the saints," with dumbwaiters to carry the food down to the church parlors.

Beecher insisted that his new church should be "substantially built, and its several parts allowed time to settle and season, each in its turn." The work was to be done by "honest, competent, conscientious workmen . . . hired at full wages, by the day." The membership of Beecher's church was less than 350, with "not six men in it who can strictly be called rich." To raise the estimated cost of fifty thousand dollars, Beecher devised a plan to secure "wholly *voluntary* and strictly *confidential*" subscriptions—a "building tax" even "more curious and surprising" than the exceedingly curious—but sensible—edifice being planned. He gave each member a printed circular enclosed in an envelope, "addressed to himself, to be returned through the post office." At the end of "a month of two," two-thirds of the circulars had come back "silently and secretly"; then, "without mentioning the name of any giver or the amount of his gift," Beecher announced from the pulpit that all of the money needed had been pledged.[88]

Here and there, other small-town and rural pastors made use of the institutional church idea. In 1888 one pastor reported having established in his rural parish "a reading and amusement room, a musical society, and an evening drawing-school." In 1889 the Reverend William Sewall, of Charlton, Massachusetts, reported holding services "on week evenings in winter and on Sabbath afternoons (four o'clock) in summer." In the 1890s, reading circles, lyceums, and temperance clubs, as well as the Grange and kindred social and fraternal organizations, were found in rural congregations.[89]

One illustration of the suburban use of the institutional ideal was found in the Congregational church at Melrose Heights, Massachusetts. "Situated in the midst of a population almost universally provided with beautiful homes, with no constituency of . . . poor people, this church might seem to have little need or opportunity for the application of the new idea." Yet this church, under the Reverend B.F. Leavitt, widened its activities according to "modern methods" to include a reading room, a gymnasium, and a debating society. Perhaps its most interesting feature was its Young Men's Christian League, "an appeal in the name of a Christianity which includes the cultivation of a complete symmetrical manhood," on the order of the Brotherhood of Andrew and Philip. The League contained "Harvard and Institute of Technology students, grocers, high school boys, painters, clerks, and carpenters," and in matters of "general public interest" its members were "leading spirits."[90]

In 1891, in the New England shoe manufacturing town of North Brookfield, the congregation that had been started by the brothers Amana and Freeman Walker, prominent in the anti-slavery movement, deliberately imported the institutional idea. It was reported that "the plan of keeping the 'meeting house' open and warm all day and evening and every day in the week [was] not in full accord with the New England ideas of economy. . . . For weeks and months no special work was attempted [but] the morning sermons were saturated with institutionalism."

Finally, the Enterprise Club was formed, to discuss various topics relating to the public welfare. Full reports were printed in the local papers. The local talent was at times supplemented by speakers from elsewhere. Although the club never credited itself with any of the changes which came about, within four years music had been introduced in the public school, the town had put in a system of water works; and money had been given by childless people to erect a free public library and reading room costing about forty thousand dollars, and a memorial church costing over sixty thousand dollars, especially adapted to institutional work.

Also, stimulated by the efforts of Senator George F. Hoar, General Francis A. Walker, the Reverend Edward Everett Hale, and others to preserve the General Rufus Putnam homestead in the neighboring town of Rutland, "a few kindred spirits known to be interested in local history" met at the pastor's house. The result was the formation of the Quaboag Historical Society, which grew to six hundred members and bound the whole region together with a common interest. A "Union League" boys' club was formed, open to Roman Catholics and Protestants alike. It was reported that although "there have been those who have reduced their church gifts because they did not approve of a gymnasium under the church, . . . the majority have caught the ideal presented and in patient self-denial have made many sacrifices of strength, time, and means to help along the work."[91]

THE "REAL FUNCTION"

Even as early as 1892 there were complaints that the institutional churches were duplicating municipal efforts, that "the institutional church provides a reading-room and library—the city has furnished these already; the institutional church opens evening classes—the city supports evening schools; the institutional church has cheap entertainments, lectures, industrial classes, a gymnasium, a dispensary—all these are to be found elsewhere in the city."[92]

The originators of the movement, however, were aware of the dangers and had anticipated the various criticisms. "Let us not be understood as advocating the degradation of the church to devices and novelties," Tucker had warned in 1886. "The power of the church cannot be revived through kitchens, parlors, entertainments, literary circles. These may have a place in the social duties of a church, but should never be confused with its real function."[93]

Institutional churches, as a rule, agreed with Tucker about the "real function." St. Bartholomew's, Berkeley Temple, and even the Jersey City Tabernacle held staunchly, in word and deed, to the view that "the supreme end of all departments" was not "mere humanitarianism" but "the spiritual life." Institutional church leader Charles S. Mills was straightforward in his simple pronouncement that the church "will entertain that she may save." University of Chicago theologian Shailer Mathews noted with satisfaction that "even more clearly" than churches of the "older sort," the "free and open" churches made religion supreme.[94]

"The range of help is as wide as the range of human necessity," wrote Charles L. Thompson when he was president of the Open and Institutional Church League in 1896, "but the supreme end always is to manifest the spirit of Christ and so draw the people to Him." As St. Bartholomew's explained it, the work of the church in winning men to Christ was simply going forward "upon old lines"; and, if some things seemed new, it was simply "that kind of newness which results from growing, and which, as it encounters new needs and emergencies, provides new methods to meet them."[95]

NOTES

1. Pentecost, "Evangelization of Our Cities. No. I," *Homiletic Review* 10 (1885): 295; idem, "Evangelization of Our Cities. No. III," ibid., 475.

2. W.H.H. Murray, "A Metropolitan Church," *Congregationalist,* 11 Dec. 1873.

3. Pentecost, "Evangelization of Our Cities. No. I," 293; Charles A. Dickinson, "Problem of the Modern City Church," *Andover Review* 12 (1889): 361; and Thomas Dixon, *The Failure of Protestantism in New York and Its Causes* (New York, 1896), p. 16.

4. Pentecost, "Evangelization of Our Cities. No. I," 295.

5. "Industrialists of the period regarded labor as a commodity—a raw material like ore or lumber to be mined of its vitality and flushed away. Profits were enormous against meager wages." Steel workers labored 12 hours a day, 7 days a week, "in 117-degree heat in a smoky, clangorous bedlam for a maximum of $1.25 a day." Drivers of horse-drawn streetcars "received $12 a week for a 16-hour day." Child labor was "a bargain at $1.50 to $2.50 a week," and "Chinese laborers . . . from the West Coast . . . were willing to work for $26 a month." By 1890, one percent of the population owned "as much as the remaining 99 percent put together." Marshall Field's income "was calculated to be $600 an hour, while his shopgirls, at a salary of $3 to $5 a week, had to work over three years to earn that amount" (Otto L. Bettmann, *The Good Old Days—They Were Terrible!* [New York, 1974], passim).

6. See, for example, "The Labor Problem," *Presbyterian,* 23 Apr. 1887; and Albion W. Small, "The Meaning of the Social Movement," *American Journal of Sociology* 3 (1897): 352, 353.

7. George E. McNeill, "State Organizations of Labor in Massachusetts," *Independent,* 2 May 1895.

8. This was a theme that ran through the entire literature of the period. See, for example, Charles Loring Brace, *Dangerous Classes of New York and Twenty Years Work among Them* (New York, 1872). Brace headed the Children's Aid Society of New York, which was engaged in rescuing street children and providing homes for them in the Midwest. By 1884, in thirty years of work, the Society had provided homes for 67,287 children, and had spent $3,426,038. It also carried on thirteen industrial schools, with fourteen thousand students ("Lay Criticism on the Ministry," *Homiletic Review* 8 [1884] 652fn).

9. Charles Richmond Henderson, "The Place and Functions of Voluntary Associations," *American Journal of Sociology* 1 (1895): 330.

10. "What the Workingmen Need," *Workingman's Advocate,* 24 June 1871.

11. "The Meeting at St. Louis," *Workingman's Advocate,* 24 June 1871. The Platform of the National Industrial Congress was printed in full in the *Workingman's Advocate,* 19 Dec. 1874, and reprinted in numerous subsequent issues of this journal.

12. C.M. Hyde, "New Times, New Men, New Methods," *Congregationalist,* 23 Oct. 1890.

13. Washington Gladden, "The Working People and the Churches," *Independent,* 23 July 1884; idem, "The Working People and the Churches," ibid., 30 July 1884. By "working people," Gladden meant "wage-workers engaged in manual labor," excluding "clerks, salesmen, . . . and small trademen." He noted as other reasons for nonattendance at church the fact that "ministers sometimes preach politics"; that workingmen "want the day for rest and refreshment"; that they "prefer to spend the day in saloons"; that they lacked suitable clothing to attend church; that the churches were snobbish and exclusive.

14. Huntington, "Some Points in the Labor Question," *Church Review* 48 (1886): 2; Pentecost, "Evangelization of Our Cities. No. I," 295; and Richards, "Labor: A Revolution and a Problem," *Lutheran Quarterly* 23 (1893): 68.

15. Rylance, *Lectures on Social Questions* (New York, 1880), cited in *American Church Review* 32 (1880): 243.

16. Smyth, "Sermon I. Claims of Labor," *Andover Review* 3 (1885): 302-312; idem, "Sermon II. Use and Abuse of Capital," ibid., 423-436; idem, "Sermon III. Social Helps," ibid., 508-519. See also William Jewett Tucker, "Social Problems in the Pulpit: Dr. Newman Smyth's Sermons to Workingmen." *Andover Review* 3 (1885): 297, 298.

17. See Charles S. Albert, "The Church and the Labor Problem," *Lutheran Quarterly* 17 (1887): 248, 249; and A. Fitzgerald Irvine, "A University Labor Union," *Outlook,* 20 Jan. 1906.

18. George Willis Cooke, "The Institutional Church," *New England Magazine* 14 (1896): 646, 647.

19. Steward L. Woodford, "Lay Criticism on the Ministry and the Methods of Church Work," *Homiletic Review* 7 (1884): 293; Darwin B. James, "Lay Criticism on the Ministry and the Methods of Church Work," ibid., 12 (1886): 216; and S.S. Cox, "Lay Criticism on the Ministry," ibid., 10 (1885): 444, 445. See also Richards, "Labor: A Revolution," 67, 68.

Notes

20. Thompson, "Symposium on the Institutional Church. I. An Agency in Accord with the Spirit and Method of the Gospel," *Homiletic Review* 32 (1896): 562; Dwight, "Lay Criticism on the Ministry," *Homiletic Review* 8 (1884): 590.

21. A.R. Quint, "Concerning Club-Houses," *Congregationalist,* 27 Mar. 1878.

22. Ely, "Socialism," *Andover Review* 5 (1886): 157, 160.

23. James Craik, "The Financial Question in the Church," *American Church Review* 38 (1882): 62; and "Facts about Pews: An Inside View of Thirty-six Churches. Taxes, Rentals, Free Seats, Annual Deficits," *Congregationalist,* 13 Feb. 1873.

24. "175 Years at Hopewell Church," *Christian Intelligencer,* 4 Jan. 1933.

25. Bridgman, "A Plea for Free Pews," *Congregationalist,* 29 May 1890.

26. John Winthrop Ballantine, "A Great Church Enterprise," *Independent,* 21 Feb. 1884.

27. Ibid.

28. Ibid.

29. See, for example, Ralph W. Brokaw, "Pews Rented or Free—Which?" *Congregationalist,* 1 June 1893; Craik, "The Financial Question," 62; Alexander McKenzie, "Free Churches," *Congregationalist,* 12 Dec. 1872; and D.K. Nesbit, "Some Advantages of the Pew Rent System" *Congregationalist,* 16 Feb. 1893.

30. Ballantine, "A Great Church Enterprise."

31. Julius H. Ward, "Utility of the Church Congress," *American Church Review* 27 (1875): 57, 58.

32. Palmer, "Contribution of the Episcopal Church to Modern Religious Life," *Andover Review* 17 (1892): 372-384.

33. Palmer, "Contribution of the Episcopal Church," 384; and "The Church and Social Questions," Louisville *Christian Observer,* 26 December 1906. See also Willem A. Visser t'Hooft, *Background of the Social Gospel in America,* Bethany Reprint (n.d., reprinted from Haarlem, 1928), p. 72.

34. Ward, "Utility of the Church Congress," 59, 61.

35. Ibid., 64, 65. See also Edgar Gardner Murphy, "Reconstruction in Religion," *Outlook,* 23 Mar. 1901.

36. "The Church Congress," *American Church Review* 28 (1876): 156.

37. The material on the Church of the Holy Communion is taken from "Fifty Years of Beginnings," *Outlook,* 19 Dec. 1896; and "A Working Church," *Christian Union,* 29 Jan. 1885. The *Outlook* claimed that this church also had the first boys' choir and the first Christmas tree in America. See also "Report of the Annual Convention of the Open and Institutional Church League," *Open Church* 3 (1899): 23. For a recent biography of Muhlenberg, see Alvin W. Skardon, *Church Leader in the Cities: William Augustus Muhlenberg* (Philadelphia, 1971).

38. The quotations are from "Free and Open Association of the Protestant Episcopal Church," *Open Church* 2 (1898): 277; and J. Macbride Sterrett, "Sociology in the West," *Churchman,* 26 Mar. 1892. See also Ely, "The Christian Social Union a Social University," *Churchman,* 26 Mar. 1892. There is a history of CAIL and of the Christian Social Union in Charles Howard Hopkins, *Rise of the Social Gospel in American Protestantism, 1865-1915* (New Haven, 1940), pp. 149-167.

39. The quotation is from "Free and Open Church Association of the Protestant Episcopal Church," 278. See also "The Free Pew System—Some of the Difficulties," *Christian Union,* 3 Jan. 1889.

40. Frank Mason North, "New Era of Church Work in the City of New York," *Christian City* 9 (1897): 10, 11.

41. This history of the Church of the Transfiguration is taken from George MacAdam, *The Little Church Around the Corner* (New York, 1925); and "Actors' Church Alliance," *Outlook,* 9 Mar. 1901.

42. The quotations are from Henry C. Bourne, "Four Institutional Churches. I. St. George's, New York," *Congregationalist,* 13 Apr. 1893; and North, "New Era of Church Work," 8.

43. The material on St. George's is taken from Bourne, "St. George's, New York"; North, "New Era of Church Work," 8-13; and Cooke, "The Institutional Church," 657. The quotation is from "A Wonderful Parish," *Churchman,* 30 Jan. 1892.

44. The material on St. Bartholomew's is taken from "Woman's Place and Work: Parish Work. V. St. Bartholomew's Church," *Churchman,* 20 Feb. 1892; "Church Club of New York," ibid., 9 Feb. 1895; and North, "New Era of Church Work," 13, 12. The quotations are from George J. Manson, "Progressive Methods of Church Work. II. Two Model Parish Houses," *Christian Union,* 21 Nov. 1891; and Cooke, "The Institutional Church," 656.

45. Tucker, "Some Present Questions in Evangelism," *Andover Review* 1 (1884): 235, 236.

46. Tucker, "Editorial," *Andover Review* 7 (1887): 80; idem, "Some Present Questions in Evangelism," 235, 236.

47. "Tolman's Square Congregational Church in London . . . stands in what was once a well-to-do locality. Now it is occupied by artisans and laborers and poorer classes. . . . It has three halls, Bands of Hope, penny concerts, evening classes, mothers' meetings, . . . and many other useful appliances. It runs smoothly and prosperously under the leadership of Rev. Mr. Hastings, who is a genius" (Raynor S. Pardington, "Symposium on the Institutional Church V. As Supplying a Need of Mixed City Life," *Homeiletic Review* 33 [1897]: 374, 375).

48. The quotations are from M.C. Ayers, "The Work of Berkeley Temple," *Christian Union,* 6 Dec. 1888; and William T. Ellis, "New Era of Church Work in Boston," *Open Church* 1 (1897): 175-177.

49. The quotations are from Ellis, "New Era of Church Work," 175, 176; "Four Institutional Churches. IV. Berkeley Temple, Boston," *Congregationalist,* 4 May 1893; Cooke, "The Institutional Church," 655; and Edmund K. Alden, "Progressive Methods of Church Work. VI. The Berkeley Temple of Today," *Outlook,* 2 Jan. 1892. See also "A Southern Institutional Church," *Congregationalist,* 14 Dec. 1893.

50. William Jewett Tucker, "Editorial," *Andover Review* 5 (1886): 70.

51. Cooke, "The Institutional Church," 648.

52. Mills, "The Institutional Church," *Bibliotheca Sacra* 49 (1892): 465; and Ward, "The Institutional Church," *Christian City* 12 (1900): 24.

53. Scudder is cited in Mills, "The Institutional Church," 457.

54. Judson, "Symposium on the Institutional Church. VI. The Institutional Church a Remedy for Social Alienation," *Homiletic Review* 33 (1897): 474.

55. Ward, "The Institutional Church," 28.

56. The quotations are from Thompson, "Symposium on the Institutional Church," 560. The "Platform of the Open and Institutional Church League" is found in *Open Church* 1 (1897): 4.

57. Moseley H. Williams, "New Era of Church Work in Philadelphia," *Open Church* 1 (1897): 67-73. See also J. Wilbur Chapman, "Bethany Church of Philadelphia," *Chautauquan* 12 (1891): 470-473.

58. John J. Foust, "A Strategic Center for a Larger Work," *Christian City* 10 (1898): 453-459.

59. E.J. Helms, "Morgan Chapel, Boston," *Christian City* 11 (1899): 62-64.

60. The quotations are from George J. Manson, "Progressive Methods of Church Work. XVI. How Rich and Poor Meet Together at Asbury Church," *Outlook,* 8 Apr. 1893. See also North, "New Era of Church Work," 15. The "pleasant Sunday afternoon" was an idea also used in England: "The motto of every P.S.A. Society is . . . 'Brief, Bright, and Brotherly,' and we arrange our service to give an object lesson in the sentiments it embodies. We meet from 3 to 4 p.m., . . . when . . . the public house is closed. . . . With the exception of the cheering and the solo singing, the service is as like an ordinary service as the proverbial 'two peas.' It is distinctly religious, and yet the workingmen swarm into it without any special effort. . . . Every seat is free—free as God's free air. . . . We are getting the class we want to reach" (A. Golden Byles, "The Pleasant Sunday Afternoon Movement in England," *Independent,* 21 Feb. 1895).

61. Williams, "New Era of Church Work," 57-59.

62. Ibid., 62-65.

63. The quotation is from North, "New Era of Church Work," 15. See also "Progressive Methods of Church Work. III. A New Departure," *Christian Union,* 5 Dec. 1891.

64. The quotations are from "Four Institutional Churches. II. The Fourth Church, Hartford," *Congregationalist,* 20 Apr. 1893; and Members of Fourth Church to Taylor, 20 July 1892, Graham Taylor Collection, Newberry Library, Chicago.

65. Henry H. Kelsey, "The Christian Industrial League," *Open Church* 1 (1897): 137, 138. See also H. Porter Dyer, "Some Great Working Churches: Hope Church, Springfield," *Congregationalist,* 4 Feb. 1886.

66. Williams, "New Era of Church Work," 60-62.

67. Emory J. Haynes, "Tremont Temple: A Church in Boston," *Chautauquan* 12 (1890): 48-51. See also "Newsboys' and Bootblacks' Thanksgiving," *Congregationalist,* 6 Dec. 1882.

68. Dickinson, "Problem of the Modern City Church," 364; Ward, "The Institutional Church," 25, 26; and Conwell, "Symposium on the Institutional Church. II. As a Factor in City Evangelization," *Homiletic Review* 33 (1897): 184.

69. Editorial comment in *Christian Union,* 21 Nov. 1891.

70. The quotations are from "Four Institutional Churches. III. The Jersey City Tabernacle," *Congregationalist,* 27 Apr. 1893; Edmund K. Alden, "Progressive Methods of Church Work. I. The Jersey City Tabernacle and People's Palace," *Christian Union,* 21 Nov. 1891; "The People's Palace of New Jersey," *Charities Review* 1 (1891): 90; and Cooke, "The Institutional Church," 658. The People's Palace in London is described in Syndney Herbert Cox, "A Genuine People's Palace," *Congregationalist and Christian World* 90 (1905): 48.

71. Sylvanus Stall, "Methods of Church Work," *Christian City* 9 (1897): 28.

72. William Ives Washburn, "The Layman's Part in Mission Work," *Congregationalist,* 15 May 1890.

73. The quotations are from "New Era of Church Work: Ruggles St. Baptist Church, Boston," *Open Church* 2 (1898): 205-212; and Everett D. Burr, "Methods of an Open and Institutional Church," ibid. 1 (1897): 98, 99.

74. "What the Churches Are Doing," *Independent,* 20 Nov. 1913; North, "New Era of Church Work," 18; and "The Judson Memorial," *Christian Union,* 21 Mar. 1889. See also Edward Judson, *Adoniram Judson: A Biography by His Son* (Philadelphia, 1902, abridged from New York, 1883); and Virgil E. Robinson, *The Judsons of Burma* (Washington, 1966).

75. The quotations are from North, "New Era of Church Work," 17, 18; and "The Judson Memorial." See also Edward Judson, *The Institutional Church: A Primer in Pastoral Theology* (New York, 1899).

76. The quotations are from "The Baptist Temple, Philadelphia," *Outlook,* 22 Feb. 1896; Moseley H. Williams, "New Era of Church Work in Philadelphia. Second Article," *Open Church* 1 (1897): 113, 114; and Edmund K. Alden, "Progressive Methods of Church Work. XV. The Temple, Philadelpha," *Outlook,* 18 Mar. 1893.

77. Williams, "New Era of Church Work," 113-115. Williams also reported that the Temple carried an insurance of $75,000 on the life of Conwell that would "wipe out the debt upon the property either at his death or at the expiration of fifteen years, the term of endowment" (Ibid., 112).

78. Ibid., 113-120. The quotation is from Alden, "Progressive Methods of Church Work. XV. The Temple, Philadelphia."

79. Cooke, "The Institutional Church," 649, 650. McCulloch's wife published a collection of his sermons under the title *The Open Door* (Indianapolis, 1892).

80. See Cooke, "The Institutional Church," 659 for a list of institutional churches. See also Simon Gilbert, "Some Great Working Churches: Plymouth Church, Minneapolis," *Congregationalist,* 18 Feb. 1886; and S.B. Kellogg, "Some Great Working Churches: Pilgrim Church, St. Louis," ibid., 11 Feb. 1886.

81. "List of Free Pew Churches," *Congregationalist,* 16 Feb. 1893; and "Annual Convention of the Open and Institutional Church League," *Christian City* 9 (1897): 35.

82. Charles Richmond Henderson, "Social Work of Chicago Churches," *Open Church* 2 (1898): 265.

83. The quotations are from Henderson, "Social Work of Chicago Churches," 265-267; and Melville E. Stone, "The Higher Life of Chicago," *Outlook,* 22 Feb. 1896.

84. Cooke, "The Institutional Church," 651, 652.

85. "Woman's Place and Work: Parish Work. VI. Grace Church, Chicago," *Churchman,* 9 Apr. 1892.

86. Charles Richmond Henderson, "New Era of Church Work: Immanuel Baptist Church, Chicago," *Open Church* 3 (1899): 11.

87. Mills, "The Institutional Church," 469; Thompson, "Symposium on the Institutional Church," 564; Ward, "The Institutional Church," 29.

88. Samuel Langhorne Clemens, "A New Beecher Church," in *A Curious Dream: and Other Sketches* (London, 1872), pp. 24-38.

89. Charles Loveland Merriam, "Problem of the Country Church," *Andover Review* 10 (1888): 393; "Problem of the Country Church: A Communication," *Andover Review* 11 (1889): 191; and "The Institutional Idea in the Country," *Congregationalist,* 10 Nov. 1892.

90. Charles S. Macfarland, "The Church and Young Men," *Christian City* 9 (1897): 37-39.

91. Joseph Jansen Spencer, "Open and Institutional Work in the Village Church: A New England Experiment," *Open Church* 3 (1899): 4-10.

92. "The Institutional Idea in the Country."

93. William Jewett Tucker, "Christianity and Its Modern Competitors. II. Social Ethics," *Andover Review* 7 (1887): 76.

94. R.Q. Mallard, "Symposium on the Institutional Church. II. Not the Ideal Church," *Homiletic Review* 33 (1897): 86; Mills, "The Institutional Church," 455; and Mathews, "Significance of the Church to the Social Movement," *American Journal of Sociology* 4 (1899): 609.

95. Thompson, "Symposium on the Institutional Church," 562; Mallard, "Symposium on the Institutional Church," 86, 87.

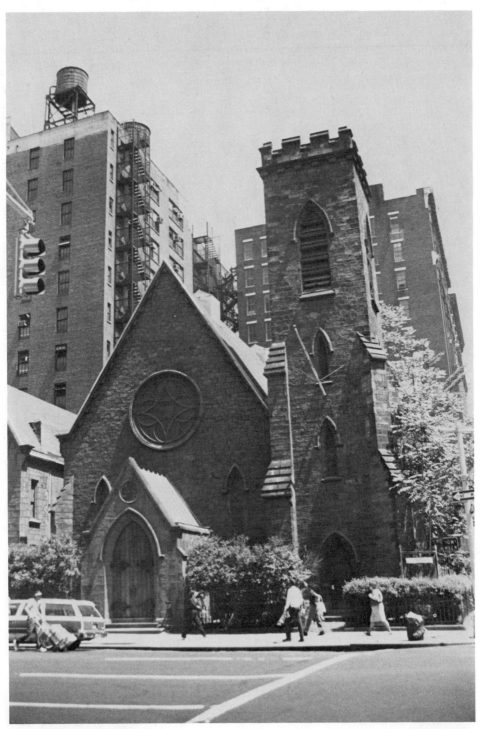

The "Church of Beginnings"
Church of the Holy Communion
Sixth Ave. and W. 20th St.
New York City

JOE STEVENS

Conversion from
Church of the Holy Communion
to the Limelight Entertainment Complex 1983

JOE STEVENS

Saint Peter's Church
Lexington Ave. and 54th St.
New York City
1861-1977

SAINT PETER'S
CHURCH ARCHIVES

Dedication of
Saint Peter's "Urban Living Room"
4 December 1977

JOHN TAYLOR
WORLD COUNCIL OF CHURCHES
GENEVA, SWITZERLAND

Saint Peter's Church
The World's "First Condominium Church"
Citicorp Center, New York City

CHAPTER THREE

Outward Visible Signs of Inward Grace: Open Church Organizations and Theology 1880-1900

Conservative clergymen were alarmed at the "hidden" proselytizing of the "free and open" churches. They maintained that "salvation from sin, with all its incoming virtues," was sufficient to make "the man better all around—a better citizen, husband, father, son, friend, toiler, trademan" and would lift "all dependent on him to a higher plane." They objected to the institutional church for putting its emphasis "where Christ and the Apostles did not—on human misery rather than human sin."[1]

"Human nature being what it is, the secular departments . . . overshadow the religious," was the judgment of one clergyman. "We have no warrant for converting the Church of God, ordained for special spiritual ends, into an *olla podrida* for all possible charities and benevolences." Even those with mixed feelings about the institutional church movement, however, were willing to admit "the purity of the motives of its advocates and the usefulness of their organizations."[2]

INSTITUTIONAL ORGANIZATIONS

Along with the institutional churches, there grew up a number of organizations and methods that spread through Protestant churches everywhere as tangible indications that American Protestantism had moved into the modern urban age. Perhaps the organization most representative of the institutional church movement, and a true child of it, was the Brotherhood of Andrew and Philip, an outgrowth of the St. Andrew's Brotherhood of the Episcopalian church. The Brotherhood was started in 1884 at St. James Church in Chicago, by twelve men under the leadership of James L. Houghteling, "a man eminently fitted for such a position by a long experience in other fields of Christian work." Its rules were two: the rule of prayer and the rule of service. Its object was to spread Christ's kingdom among young men. The members were "pledged to pray every day for this, and to make an honest effort to bring at least one young man during the week under the influence of the gospel."[3]

The young men of Bethany Presbyterian Church, Philadelphia, for example, did "everything in their power to be faithful to their pledge." They opened a reading room and gymnasium; they provided themselves with invitations to all the services of the church, and gave them out wherever possible; they scattered through the church during the service, "that they may welcome the stranger, . . . help the one who may seem to be impressed; . . . go with him to the after-meeting."[4]

At St. George's in New York, the Brotherhood of St. Andrew took over the work of Epiphany House in Stanton Street, in 1891, after nine clergymen in as many years "had undertaken the work of the mission and . . . given it up." The Brotherhood formed a new board of trustees, agreed to raise six thousand dollars a year to carry on the work, and placed one of their members, Charles J. Wills, in charge.[5]

Equally extensive was the King's Daughters, formed 13 January 1886 by some Christian ladies in New York. There were ten at the meeting. This first ten comprised the Central Council, through which the business of the organization was conducted under the presidency of Mrs. Margaret Bottome, the wife of a well-known Methodist clergyman in the city of New York. Any lady could join the order, gather nine women around her, and then secure the formation of other "Tens" around the initial group. There were "Tens" that sang in hospitals and prisons, "Tens" of young girls who supported orphan children, sewing "Tens," and "Tens" formed by ladies who desired "to discipline their tongues and tempers."[6]

The Boys' Brigade, "taking advantage of that passion for . . . military life which is rarely asleep in a boy's breast," was an import from Scotland, where it was founded in 1883 by William A. Smith, an officer of the First Lanarkshire Rifle Volunteers, "the crack corps of the city of Glasgow." A few men met in January 1885 at Smith's home in Glasgow to draw up a constitution for the Boys' Brigade. "A great and splendid discovery," it first appeared in America as the creation of a Reverend Russell, who organized his first company at the Tabernacle Church in Kansas City in 1890.[7]

The Girls' Friendly Society, founded in England in 1875, first appeared in America at Trinity Church in Newark, New Jersey, on 18 February 1885. It specialized in holiday houses for working girls. Perhaps the most famous was the Milford Holiday House of the Girls' Friendly Society of Massachusetts, three miles from the town of Milford, New Hampshire. Membership in some branch of the Girls' Friendly Society was a prerequisite to admission to the Holiday House.[8]

The first kitchen-garden was "the invention, or perhaps the discovery of Miss Emily Huntington, . . . who had lived among the thrifty, capable housewives of New England." It was apparently a cooking school in Boston opened in 1879 by the Women's Educational Association, in the belief that "reforms work easily from the upper classes downwards" and that "good cooking is a strong home influence" that would make the homes of the poor more attractive and keep the fathers from the liquor saloon. Efforts were made, for example, to introduce chocolate and cocoa as cheaper and more nutritious than tea and coffee, but "the old bake-shop habit" was not easily broken, and the results were discouraging.[9]

In 1880 the incorporators of the first kitchen-garden formed the Kitchen-Garden Association, to promote the teaching of "industrial domestic arts." In its first season the Association enrolled eighty active members and supervised the instruction of 990 children in and near New York. Four years later it realized "that the field in which it had begun must be more and more widely extended" and reorganized as the Industrial Education Association, credited with the addition of vacation schools, kindergartens, sewing classes, and manual-training high schools to the public school system. To the work of this Association are also due the Teachers' College of New York City, the Burnham Industrial School, and Pratt and Drexel Institutes.[10]

In 1897 the kindergarten of the church was called a "new departure," made imperative by overcrowding in the first grades of the public schools, an activity through which the church could condition the "power of environment" and "make it minister to the development of sincere, courageous, thoughtful Christian boys and girls." One of the most famous kindergartens was the Alfred Corning Clark Neighborhood House in Rivington Street. It carried on kindergarten work in order to "civilize" the "polyglot world" around it. It had accommodations for five hundred children, a roof garden, and living quarters for its teachers. Another well-known kindergarten was the Gerard Memorial Kindergarten at the City Park Branch of the First Presbyterian Church in Brooklyn, New York.[11]

By 1897 there was an interdenominational Kindergarten of the Church Association, with Methodist bishop John H. Vincent as president. The famed founder of Chautauqua, Vincent was a strong supporter of the institutional church. In 1892 he wrote that "we need a church opened every day, and wise provision for week-day contact with the people we would elevate and save." He asserted that the power of the minister "is in his wisdom"; that the minister "should seek to build up permanent institutions of help" and should have "words of *consolation* for the rich as well as the poor"; that the minister "stands between conflicting classes, and belongs to all."[12]

The Christian Endeavor, which by 1906 had over sixty-seven thousand societies in over fifty countries, with nearly four million members, began in 1881 as one society with forty members. Its principles were "deep religious devotion, . . . service for all and all for service [and] 'Fellowship with Fidelity.' " It was "a bridge between child nurture and adult public confession of faith."[13]

THEOLOGY OF THE INSTITUTIONAL CHURCH

Along with their polishing of refined definitions of the institutional church, the busy pastors of such churches sometimes paused to reflect on the theological rationale for their work, and the spiritual import of what they were doing. In great contrast to the multitudinous, bustling, worldly activities exhibited in these churches day by day, their theology was marked by a tender simplicity and great spiritual depth. "This movement calls all its workers to an individual Calvary," said Ward. "Its symbol is that abandoned token, the cross, as the sign of service. It has laid hold of the essential truth that the only hope for social salvation is through the redemptive quality of personal sacrifice."[14]

"The church must be sacramental; that is, it must freely employ outward and visible signs of an inward and spiritual grace. . . . The sacramental idea of shadowing forth spiritual truth by visible types and symbols ought to govern," wrote another in 1888.[15] To find that "spiritual truth" and "inward grace," institutional church pastors looked to the New Testament and there easily made connections with their work.[16]

Dickinson wrote in 1889, "We hear a great deal said about preaching the simple gospel, . . . but what is the gospel? The gospel is preaching plus practice, truth plus life. . . .

"Not that the church should conform to the world, but that it should be all things to all men in the true Pauline sense, that by all means it may save some. . . . Religion pure and undefiled is not that which remains intact only so long as it is not in contact with the world; but it is that which keeps unspotted in the dust and din of life. . . . It calls nothing common or unclean which concerns the betterment of humanity."[17]

In spite of its thus harking back to the New Testament, the institutional church was, even more, a lavish empirical outpouring of the peculiarly American "Gospel of Wealth," a gospel which owed its name and basic delineation to Andrew Carnegie. In June and December of 1889, Carnegie published two articles in the *North American Review* under the titles "Wealth," and "The Best Fields of Philanthropy." These were taken up by the *Pall Mall Gazette* in England and republished under the more striking title "The Gospel of Wealth."

"The course of discussion which had followed until now the republication of these articles is quite as significant as the original articles," wrote Tucker in 1891, and then summarized Carnegie's position as follows:

> The present economic system, which is established in individualism and worked out through competition, is on the whole the best attainable system. The millionaire is the necessary product of that system; wealth inevitably falls . . . into the hands of a few. . . . The millionaire is the natural trustee of the poor; and he can administer wealth for the community better than the community can administer it for itself. The sole question then is, How can the rich man fulfill his trusteeship? . . .
>
> Mr. Carnegie's first answer to the question . . . is, that nothing above a competence should remain in a rich man's family. . . .
>
> Mr. Carnegie's second answer is, that fortunes should not be devised by will, partly because of the uncertainty, attending all bequests, of actually reaching and accomplishing their ends, and partly because the act of bequeathing property is in itself destitute of any moral quality. . . .
>
> In Mr. Carnegie's third answer he states his positive principle that all private wealth . . . should be distributed back into society during the lifetime of the owner . . . and according to his direction, . . . specifying, as the proper objects of benevolence, universities, libraries, hospitals, parks, churches of the more costly type, and in the general those intermediate objects which enrich a community without pauperizing individuals.[18]

In the twilight of America's Gilded Age, Carnegie's words fell like a golden melody upon the ears of beleaguered capitalists who were being criticized on all sides, and especially by workingmen, for their supposedly unscrupulous business practices and for their "grinding the faces of the poor" in their greedy and heady race to wealth, and pastors sympathetic to capitalists who were mainstays in their congregations were quick to give the Gospel of Wealth a definitely Christian cast.[19]

In 1890, for example, the Cleveland Congregational Club listened with "profound interest" to a "timely and valuable" paper on the "Power of Christian Money," read by the Reverend Irving W. Metcalf, in which he said:

> The United States is the richest nation in the world. Its wealth has trebled since 1860. . . . Twelve billions of dollars, increasing at the rate of more than a million dollars a day, represents the present money power of American Christians. . . . Our American wealth is the cleanest money in the world's history. It is not wealth gotten by vanity; it is not the spoil of war. It has been gathered by the hand.
>
> The money-making power of this country is a part of God's plan for redeeming the world. Some men are as plainly called to make money for the kingdom as others are to preach it. . . . The Bible is the best text-book in the world on political economy and practical finance. Nearly all our Savior's parables refer to our relationship to property. . . . A communistic distribution will not Christianize the money power. . . . Three words represent the law of nature and the law of Christ—trusteeship, service, self-denial. . . .
> There is money enough in the hands of Christian people to evangelize the

world, and if it does not evangelize the world, it will destroy the church.[20]

In the same year, an editorial appeared in the *Congregationalist* which declared:

> There is only one possible justification for a man's possessing his thousands and his millions today, when the world is so full of unrelieved want and woe. It is the entire dedication of his purse to the service of his fellowmen in the name of Him who abandoned all His riches to become like one of us. . . . Years ago, that keen discerner of the times and seasons, that hopeful soul, Horace Bushnell, said: 'What we are waiting for, and are longing hopefully to see, is the consecration of the vast money power of the world to the work and cause and kingdom of Jesus Christ; for that day, when it comes, will be the morning of a new creation.'[21]

Suggestions of the Gospel of Wealth, actually, had appeared in Protestant sermons and publications as early as 1885. In the third of his famous sermons to workingmen, entitled "Social Helps," delivered at the Center Church in New Haven, Newman Smyth had said that "we are, none of us, largely successful, thoroughly happy or safe, if we seek only the things which are our own, if we are without public spirit, if we are not lovers of the city. The man who makes himself and his means a useful factor . . . in . . . the city's prosperity, who opens a park, . . . founds a free library or builds a hospital, or contributes in any sensible way to the happiness of the people . . . is the true socialist, the genuine reformer."[22]

On 20 December 1885, from his Indianapolis pulpit McCulloch commented on the "cold, passionless, automatic life" of Cornelius Vanderbilt, "the richest man in the world," and contrasted him with Peter Cooper and Stephen Girard. McCulloch's thesis was that "wealth is a trust," and that "the welfare of humanity must be the ideal which men should value more highly than material wealth." In the same month, a writer in the *Homiletic Review* insisted that Christian riches "are not wrung by threats, nor beguiled by ghostly devices from the dying clutch of robber-barons, but fall like ripened fruit from healthful boughs, as the intelligent and grateful surrender to its rightful owner of increase earned as stewards in His service."[23]

"By some it is held that a rich Christian is an anomaly," wrote the Reverend James M. Buckley, the powerful Methodist editor of the New York *Christian Advocate,* in 1892, but "this view is not ours," for "the blessing of the Lord sometimes maketh rich in the literal sense of the words. . . . The duty, therefore, of the Christian is to reflect how he can use his wealth to promote the kingdom of Christ." Another clergyman called "giving for Christianity or any humane work" a "glory" that "develops manhood," and added that "no man has a right to be a moral dwarf"; that "every man ought to be as manlike as possible."[24]

Thoughtful Christian laymen who added their comments to the torrent emphasized the notes of consecration and service. President Merrill E. Gates of Amherst College called wealth "concentrated power of service," and Robert C. Ogden (a "robber baron" of the Gilded Age) wrote that "the administration of money is a sacred trust demanding consecration of head and heart. To do it wisely is a science, and with grace a fine art. The Christian should be the scientist and artist of benevolence—his confession of Christ permits nothing less. . . . Given the foundation of personal consecration, . . . the cheap cant about sacrifice will cease, only to be replaced by the joy of privilege."[25]

The institutional church, without doubt, was in large part shaped by wealthy Christian laymen who saw in it the ideal place to express their genuine Christian consecration, prove their Christian manhood, and practice "the science and art of benevolence." In the institutional churches the Gospel of Wealth was empirically and manifoldly carried out. Behind St. George's was the mighty power—spiritual, moral, and financial—of J. Pierpont Morgan. Behind Ruggles Street Baptist was D.S. Ford, the proprietor of the *Youth's Companion*. St. Bartholomew's had its Vanderbilts; Bethany in Philadelphia, its Wanamaker; Plymouth Church in Chicago, its Armour, and the list went on and on.[26]

So well did these "stewards of wealth" carry out their Christian commitment that in 1912, in retrospect, John A. Ryan, the Roman Catholic exponent of Populist and Reform Darwinian thought, was to call the Christian Gospel of Wealth "by far the most distinctive and most fruitful social doctrine of Christianity," a doctrine that had "diminished selfishness and promoted the conception of wealth as a social possession and a social responsibility.[27]

Let it not be inferred, however, that the institutional churches were sustained entirely by men of wealth. The free and open churches were also an American expression—geared to its time and place—of a Christian doctrine more ancient and basic than the Gospel of Wealth, namely the doctrine of "no priestly caste," of "one great ministry, requiring service, consecrated service, from every member."[28] This "theology of the laity" received new impetus during the second half of the nineteenth century, for the reason that the clergy no longer occupied the same relative rank of superiority in intelligence and literary culture that had characterized it a century earlier. As one writer expressed it, the American clergyman had been "remanded to the ranks of ordinary citizenship."[29]

"So long as the church had independent revenues, she could afford to ignore the opinions of the laity," explained one writer in 1884, but "the increased power of the laity in the temporal affairs of the church gives them boldness and opportunity to assert an influence in matters of doctrine." The laity did, indeed, increasingly begin to express itself, especially in Sunday schools and in the religious press of the day, where "the right and ability of laymen to influence religious opinion" was fully recognized.[30]

Also in 1884 the *Homiletic Review* declared that "the *real workers*—not the talkers, the agitators, the critics and croakers—but the actual, active, patient workers" were Christian men and women, an "army of Good Samaritans . . . busy, night and day, in summer and winter, in public and in private, in all our jails and prisons and almshouses and hospitals, in all our alleys and tenement house districts, 'reeking with filth,' not only gauging the poverty and wretchedness and crime and suffering of the masses, but by a thousand systematic methods, and by ten thousand pitying hearts and liberal hands," administering relief.[31]

In 1890 the *Congregationalist* challenged the Christian layman to "seize upon his birthright, and take an active part in the management of our benevolent organizations"; and to "identify himself more especially with some one branch of Christian work," since the laity, and the laity alone, was the "source of supply" that could achieve a "perfect mechanism" of Christian social service, through conservation of forces, "federalization" of societies, and sound finance. In the free and open churches, the laity took up this challenge, so that in the 1890s many institutional church pastors, such as Charles H. Parkhurst, the controversial president of the Society for the Prevention of Crime in New York, gladly admitted that "the implement of traction, stronger than chimes, advertisements, seasoned preaching, cheap pews or hospitable ushers is . . . the agency of the lay Christians." All in all, the institutional church was, primarily, a spontaneous and vigorous American expression of the Protestant doctrine of the "priesthood of all believers.'' As such, the movement stands like a shining, shimmering star in the history of American Protestantism.[32]

EVALUATION OF THE MOVEMENT

How shall we evaluate the institutional church? It had, of course, its weaknesses and inadequacies, recognized even by those within the movement, and many criticized it negatively. It is, moreover, "impossible to determine what the institutional church meant to the people it served," or to ascertain the real extent of the movement. In 1872 such churches were reported to be "no novelty or rarity among us," and yet as late as 1897 it was also reported that "free pews are still the exception rather than the rule." The movement was endorsed by the National Congregational Council of Churches and the Quadrennial Conference of the Methodist Episcopal Church; in 1897 it was reported that "while the great majority of Protestant Episcopal and Methodist Episcopalian, and very many of the Baptist churches are free, the majority of Presbyterian churches are not." There is no doubt, however, that the newer methods found expression "in all parts of the country, and in many forms."[33]

The three main objections to the institutional church—made both from within and without the movement—were "the financial expense involved in maintaining such a church, the complexity of the organization, and the materialistic tendencies of the plan." Institutional features greatly increased the cost of church work. They made immense demands on the energy, care, and organizing ability of the leaders. Walter A. Rauschenbusch, who was to become the leading theologian of the Social Gospel, called the institutional church "a necessary evil" and complained that "the people ought to be able to provide for themselves what the churches are trying to provide for them." The caustic judgment of Amos G. Warner, representing the social work profession, was that "some pastors continue relief work long after they are discouraged about it, . . . because they do now know at what else to employ their young people and benevolent old women of both sexes."[34]

Early in the movement, however, its leaders gave simple and clear answers to the main objections. Dickinson declared that the necessary expenses were not large when the number of workers and the amount of work accomplished were taken into account. As to the objection of "too much machinery," he noted that previously the churches had lacked system and organization. He also maintained that "while it is true" that institutional work deals with "material interests and secular means," it is "taken for granted" that "back of all, and working through all, is the regenerating power of the Holy Spirit."[35]

NOTES

1. R.Q. Mallard, "Symposium on the Institutional Church. II. Not the Ideal Church," *Homiletic Review* 33 (1897): 84.

2. Ibid., 86.

3. The quotations are from Edwin J. Gardiner, "Church Work among Young Men," *Church Review* 49 (1887): 593; and J. Wilbur Chapman, "Bethany Church of Philadelphia," *Chautauquan* 12 (1891): 471.

4. Chapman, "Bethany Church of Philadelphia," 471.

5. "Epiphany House, Stanton Street, New York," *Churchman*, 5 Nov. 1892. Other churches reporting a "Brotherhood of Andrew and Philip" or a "Brotherhood of St. Andrew" included Berkeley Temple; St. Bartholomew's; Holland Memorial; Fourth Church, Hartford; Central Congregational, Philadelphia; First Presbyterian, Germantown; Messiah Parish House, Brooklyn; and the Church House, Philadelphia.

6. "The King's Daughters," *Presbyterian*, 30 July 1887. Berkeley Temple reported having six circles of the King's Daughters (William T. Ellis, "New Era of Church Work in Boston," *Open Church* 1 [1897]: 177). Other churches reporting circles included Cornell Memorial; Holland Memorial; St. Bartholomew's; St. George's; Jersey City Tabernacle; Bethany Presbyterian, Philadelphia; Grace Temple, Philadelphia; and Bethlehem, Los Angeles.

7. The quotations are from Henry C. Bourne, "Four Institutional Churches. I. St. George's, New York," *Congregationlist*, 13 Apr. 1893; and Ewing W. Hamlen, "How We Founded the Boys' Brigade," *Independent*, 18 Apr. 1895. See also James M. Campbell, "Progressive Methods of Church Work. VIII. Two Representative Missions of Chicago," *Outlook*, 27 Feb. 1892. Churches reporting a Boys' Brigade included Berkeley Temple; St. George's; Mt. Morris Baptist; First Baptist; Philadelphia; Grace Temple, Philadelphia; Old Fifth St. Church, Philadelphia; Holland Memorial; Middle Collegiate, New York; Messiah Parish House, Brooklyn; Ninth St. Baptist, Cincinnati; Immanuel Baptist, Chicago; and Armour Mission.

8. "The Girls' Friendly Society," *Christian Union*, 16 July 1885; and "The Milford Holiday House," *Churchman*, 17 Sept. 1898. Churches with societies included St. George's; St. Bartholomew's; Grace Church, Chicago; and the Church House, Philadelphia. Plymouth Church, Brooklyn, reported a "Working-Girls' Central Club" ("Progressive Methods of Church Work. V. Week-Day Work in a City Church," *Outlook*, 2 Jan. 1892).

9. The quotations are from Laura Winnington, "The Kitchen-Garden," *Outlook*, 4 May 1901; and O.M.E. Rowe, "The Ethics of the Cooking Schools," *Congregationalist*, 26 Apr. 1882. The discouraging results of this activity were underscored by Owen Kildare, author of *My Mamie Rose*, who began life as a Bowery waif; was adopted by an Irish couple living in a Catherine Street tenement; was forced into the streets again at the age of nine; and rose to become a successful author and playwright after an East Side school teacher whom he met at the age of thirty kindled within him the spark of ambition. He commented in retrospect, "I have been told that a home, improved in tone by 'advanced' mothers and children, cannot fail to reform the father. . . . I so far have failed to see it. . . . The fathers are either treated with mild and condescending contempt, or are shown that they are a cause of shame to their progeny, or are practically driven from the home. A greed for learning and advancement has sprung up which has usurped many home functions" (Kildare, "The Slums' Point of View," *Independent*, 22 June 1905).

10. Winnington, "The Kitchen-Garden." See also "Pratt Institute: A Great Industrial School," *Lutheran Observer*, 27 June 1890; and "Pratt Institute, Brooklyn, New York: Its Aim and Scope," ibid., 20 July 1894.

11. The quotation is from William W. Foster, "The Kindergarten of the Church," *Open Church* 1 (1897): 84, 85. See also "The Ministry of a Brooklyn Church," *Christian City* 10 (1898): 342-345. Rivington Street contained two magnificent public school buildings that stood "like bulwarks of the nation planted solidly in the midst of this complex life"; the Mills Hotel—the "poor man's glory"—"rearing its spacious bulk" above the "puny but populous" tenements around it; the University Settlement, "a beautiful, well-'appointed building"; and the College settlement "exerting its influence" ("One Down-Town Street," *Christian City* 11 [1899]: 19, 20). Churches with kindergartens included Morgan Chapel, Boston; Cornell Memorial; Central Congregational, Philadelphia; Immanuel Baptist, Chicago; and Armour Mission.

12. The Kindergarten of the Church Association is mentioned in Foster, "The Kindergarten of the Church," 89. See also John H. Vincent, "The Coming Church," *Independent*, 7 July 1892; idem, "The Minister and Social Problems. I," ibid., 17 Mar. 1892; idem, "The Minister and Social Problems. II," ibid., 24 Mar. 1892, from which the quotation is taken.

13. The quotations are from Francis E. Clark, "A Quarter-Century of Christian Endeavor," *Outlook,* 6 Jan. 1906; and James W. Cooper, "Child Nurture in the Church," *Andover Review* 2 (1884): 56, 57. See also Clark, "The Origin and Growth of the Christian Endeavor Movement," *Independent,* 7 July 1892; Theodore L. Cuyler, "Forerunners of the Christian Endeavor Society," ibid.; William T. Ellis, "Christian Endeavor and Higher Education," *Independent,* 18 Apr. 1895; Samuel D. Virgin, "The Christian Endeavor Movement," *Congregationalist,* 24 Apr. 1890; and John Wanamaker, "A Testimony to the Endeavor Movement," Independent, 7 July 1892. At the time, Wanamaker was Postmaster General of the United States and stated that he was "one of the original trustees of the Christian Endeavor organization."

14. Harry F. Ward, "The Institutional Church," *Christian City* 12 (1900): 28.

15. John Tunis, "Problem of the Country Church," *Andover Review* 10 (1888): 225.

16. See, for example, John 10:37, 38; Acts 6:1; and Rev. 21:22-26.

17. Charles A. Dickinson, "Problem of the Modern City Church," *Andover Review* 12 (1889): 359, 360, 371.

18. Tucker noted that Carnegie's argument made "the inevitable factor in society . . . not so certainly the poor as the rich. The rich ye have with you always," [in contrast to the Biblical adage that "the poor ye have with you always"]. Tucker opposed Carnegie's thesis for the reasons that it would fail to reach irresponsible wealth, that it amounted to patronage, that "it comes too late for a social remedy," since the problem of economic civilization "is not pauperism, . . . but the concentration of wealth [in private hands]. He pointed out ethical tendencies that were operating to prevent the concentration of wealth, such as recognition of "the moral element involved in consumption," progressive taxation of estates, and enlargement of the economic functions of the municipality and state ("The Gospel of Wealth," *Andover Review* [1891]: 633-643). Significantly, by 1901, Carnegie had revised his theory to the extent that he called the unequal distribution of wealth "temporary." (See "The Gospel of Wealth," *Outlook,* 9 Mar. 1901).

19. For a critical treatment of the Gilded Age, see H. Wayne Morgan, ed., *The Gilded Age: A Reappraisal* (Syracuse, 1963).

20. Irving W. Metcalf, "Christian Money," *Congregationalist,* 13 Nov. 1890.

21. "The Consecration of Wealth," *Congregationalist,* 17 Apr. 1890.

22. Smyth, "Sermon III. Social Helps," *Andover Review* 3 (1885): 517, 518.

23. Genevieve C. Weeks, "Religion and Social Work as Exemplified in the Life of Oscar C. McCulloch," *Social Service Review* 39 (1965): 42, 43; and Jesse B. Thomas, "Symposium on the Pulpit," *Homiletic Review* 10 (1885): 498, 499.

24. Buckley, "The Proper Uses of Christian Wealth," *Independent,* 7 Jan. 1892; and Robert S. MacArthur, "The Right Use of Wealth," ibid.

25. Gates, "The Christian's Dilemma as to Accumulation," *Independent,* 7 Jan. 1892; and Ogden, "Money and Christianity," ibid. See "Lay Criticism on the Ministry," *Homiletic Review* 8 (1884): 653 for a list of Christian laymen who left behind "numerous memorials of their beneficence and skill and work, . . . in libraries, hospitals, unions, dispensaries, lectures, and associations, to instruct and benefit the future generations." The Gospel of Wealth was also the theme of a number of Christian social novels of the period, such as Mrs. Kingley's *The Needle's Eye* (1902) and *The Singular Miss Smith* (1904); Bradford's *Between Two Masters;* and Charles M. Sheldon's *His Brother's Keeper.*

26. See William S. Rainsford, *Story of a Varied Life: An Autobiography* (New York, 1922), pp. 277-292; and "New Era of Church Work: Ruggles St. Baptist Church, Boston," 213. Dickinson's "experiment" at Berkeley Temple was initially financed with five thousand dollars pledged by the church; five thousand dollars from the Swett Fund for city evangelization; eighty-five hundred dollars from "persons in the *Youth's Companion* office, representing most generously the interest of the Baptist denomination" ("Readjustment of City Churches," *Andover Review* 9 [1888]: 77, 78).

27. Review of Charles S. Loch, *Charity and Social Life* (New York, 1910), in *American Journal of Sociology* 17 (1912): 704. For a history of the role played by John A. Ryan in the development of American Catholic social thought, see Aaron Ignatius Abell, *American Catholicism and Social Action: A Search for Social Justice, 1865-1900* (New York, 1960); and Eric F. Goldman, *Rendezvous with Destiny,* Vintage Edition (1956, abridged from New York, 1952), pp. 85,86.

28. M.H. Buckham, "Lay Theology," *Andover Review* 1 (1884): 152.

29. A.J.F. Behrends, "Symposium on the Pulpit. No V," *Homiletic Review* 10 (1885): 378, 379. In contrast, in 1800 "the pastors of the churches were looked upon with a certain awe. And to a man they felt the dignity of their station, and magnified their office. It was seldom that they were not consciously on dress parade. . . . The word *reverend* was the favorite adjective" (J.R. Duryee, "The Christian Ministry of New York at the Beginning and End of the Nineteenth Century," *Christian City* 10 [1898]: 428). Even as late as the 1890s it was reported that "a majority of our college presidents are ministers [and] of the books issued annually from the press no other single profession produces so many as the ministry" ("Points from Pulpit and Press," *Independent,* 1 Mar. 1894).

30. Buckham, "Lay Theology," 156.

31. "Lay Criticism on the Ministry," *Homiletic Review* 8 (1884): 653.

32. "Editorial," *Andover Review* 5 (1886): 71; and Parkhurst, "Lay Ministry in New York," *Independent,* 9 Jan. 1890.

33. The quotations are from Weeks, "Religion and Social Work," 51, 52; Alexander McKenzie, "Free Churches," *Congregationalist,* 12 Dec. 1872; Moseley H. Williams, "New Era of Church Work in Philadelphia. Second Article," *Open Church* 1 (1897): 118; Frank Mason North, "New Era of Church Work in the City of New York," *Christian City* 9 (1897): 14; and George Willis Cooke, "The Institutional Church," *New England Magazine* 14 (1896): 652. See also Rayner S. Pardington, "Symposium on the Institutional Church. V. As Supplying a Need of Mixed City Life," *Homiletic Review* 33 (1897): 374. The Lutheran denomination in America was largely composed of immigrants and therefore not in the main stream of the institutional church movement. One writer described it as "the most polyglot church in America," with 1,378,776 members, a dozen languages, and an "extraordinary" parochial school system; and lauded it for doing "ten times" as much work with the immigrants as "all other denominations together" (George H. Schodde, "Work among the Immigrants," *Independent,* 7 Mar. 1895).

34. Dickinson, "Problem of the Modern City Church," 370; Rauschenbusch, "The Church in the Social Movement," *American Journal of Sociology* 3 (1897): 25, 26; and Warner "Our Charities and Our Churches," *Proceedings of the Sixteenth National Conference of Charities and Correction* (1889), p. 39.

35. Mallard, "Symposium on the Institutional Church," 86; and Dickinson, "Problem of the Modern City Church," 370, 371.

CHAPTER FOUR

The Church as a "Useful Maid-of-All-Work":
Defining the Social Role of the Church
1885-1912

The clergy and laity of institutional churches readily admitted, and outside observers agreed, that their primary goal was evangelism. At the People's Palace in New Jersey, John L. Scudder declared with pride that "conversion is the goal of all our organizations. . . . The whole drift is toward the kingdom of God, and [newcomers] are soon made to feel it, and are swept along unconsciously by it."[1]

Some of the free and open churches, such as Beacon Presbyterian in Philadelphia and St. Bartholomew's in New York, made strenuous efforts to keep their "accessories" separate from the "regular work of the church," but all of the institutional churches without exception emphasized the evangelistic "after-meeting." Graham Taylor's Fourth Church, in Hartford, Connecticut, was known as a "soul saving center." In Boston, Tremont Temple had its "anxious seat" and Ruggles Street Baptist its "gospel wagon." The "new method of bettering man's earthly conditions, educating and entertaining him, giving him better rates than the money-broker, clothing him" had all been added as additional "means of favorably impressing him with the Gospel remedy for sin and wretchedness."[2]

In spite of a strong evangelistic emphasis, however, and in spite of elaborate educational and welfare programs and lavish use of manpower and money, socially minded Protestant church leaders were to come to the conclusion that the free and open church—just as the traditional mission chapel it had sought to supplant—was unsuccessful in winning members to the church. In 1894 William S. Rainsford, the indefatigable rector of St. George's in New York, declared flatly that "the mission chapel feature of our modern Christianity is failure from beginning to end." The enormous amounts of money, manpower, and intense social service that St. George's had poured into the "pitiful wilderness of human life below Fourteenth Street" had not changed that sense of failure. At a meeting summoned by the Episcopalian bishop of New York to consider the best methods of carrying on church work on the East Side, Rainsford, the principal speaker, sadly concluded that "we cannot do much with the people over twenty-five years old. Here and there you will fill the churches, but it cannot be done except you give them tea and toast, and then if you stop the tea and toast they disappear; as soon as the tea is cold they go."[3]

THE CHASM BETWEEN CHURCH AND LABOR

The free and open churches did not succeed in gaining the interest and support of working men. Organized labor, in general, rebuffed the efforts of the churches to reach workingmen, who continued to reiterate the same complaints about the churches that they had made in the 1870s. In 1892, for example, the Massachusetts Congregational Association appointed a Committee on the Work of the Churches, to inquire "whether industrial discontent has produced any effect upon the attitude of the workingmen in Massachusetts toward the churches." Enquiries were sent both to ministers and to representatives of labor societies, and the answers from the latter were "suspicious, . . . satirical or contemptuous" and conflicted with those of the ministers. As in the past, laborers charged that the churches were allied with, and subservient to, the "oppressing class," meaning the employers of labor, and capitalists in general.[4]

Near the beginning of the twentieth century, a new and dynamic would-be peacemaker between church and labor appeared on the Protestant scene in the person of the Reverend Charles Stelzle. Stelzle, after serving an apprenticeship of five years in the shops of the Hoe Printing Press Company in New York City and laboring for three years as a unionist workingman, entered the Moody Institute in Chicago to study for the ministry, "with the particular purpose of working among day-laborers." In 1897 he was called to Hope Chapel, a mission of Westminster Presbyterian Church in north Minneapolis. Stelzle reported that nearly one-half of the 290 saloons in the city were within thirteen blocks of his chapel. He developed Hope Chapel into a viable institutional church, with a boys' club for newsboys and bootblacks, "many of them being the breadwinners for the family"; an industrial school, a free dispensary, and the largest known kindergarten in the Midwest; concerts and lectures, and "meetings in the interest of broad philanthropic movements." Within a year the monthly attendance was nearly ten thousand.[5]

From Minneapolis, Stelzle was called to New York City to take charge of the Hope Chapel there. Then he went to the Menard Street Mission in St. Louis. From there, in 1901, he sent out two hundred copies of a circular letter to labor leaders asking, "What is the chief fault that workingmen find with the Church?" He reported that "nearly every labor leader" replied that "the Church is not for the poor man; . . . it is a rich man's club"; it is "organized hypocrisy" deviating from "the religion of Jesus."[6]

Even a former workingman such as Stelzle seemed unable to do much to change the negative view of workingmen about the church. The reason lay partly in the fact that even Protestant clergymen sympathetic to laboring men and women spoke of them with suspicion and condescension. In 1886, Episcopalian bishop Frederic Dan Huntington had taken the position that the "difficulties" were "further aggravated" by the character of the immigrant. "Among them," he declared, "are men and women of turbulent dispositions, of reckless passions, desperate, besotted, brutish, incapable of reflection,— the vicious material of which mobs are always made." Huntington and others also spoke against the "menacing attitude" and the brutal tactics of the Knights of Labor, and the institutional churches openly opposed the severe apprenticeship restrictions set up by labor unions against Chinese and other foreign labor. One of the main reasons why most institutional churches sponsored industrial and trade schools was the fact that young people and illiterate immigrants often could get no training under the auspices of labor unions.[7]

Perhaps a more basic reason for the alienation of labor from the church could be found, however, in the fact that *capital* and *labor* were *not* two distinct concepts in the minds of most Protestant clergymen. In 1872 liberal Congregational theologian Theodore T. Munger had written that a laborer may do "very well as an animal, but very poorly as a man." He characterized the condition of labor as "slavery"; yet, inconsistently, he concluded that "we do not recognize *sides.*" He insisted that labor's salvation lay not in antagonism to capital, but in alliance with capital; not in *"fighting* Capital," but in *"getting* Capital." Even as late as 1894, many Protestant pastors still insisted that "there is no such distinction as is implied in the terms capital *and* labor." One wrote in the *Presbyterian,* "Labor and capital ever stand related, as root and fruit. . . . What is capital? Labor. What is labor? Capital. What is cheese but milk? What is milk but potential cheese?"[8]

Protestant clergymen continued to hold firmly to the entrenched Ricardian thought of the nineteenth century which insisted that economic laws were immutable, and that the "iron law of wages" was God given and sacred. Munger, thus, ominously predicted for labor "no future . . . but endless strikes." He explained that the laboring classes "see clearly that there is an impassable gulf between their poverty and the results of their toil," but that "apparently they do not consider the inexorable logic of the economic laws that regulate wages and prices."[9]

Such belief was not questioned even in the academic world in American until after 1885, when Richard T. Ely, Simon Nelson Patten, and other economists began to advance the startling new idea that economic laws are relative—evolving out of time, place, and nationality—and within the control of man. The Protestant point of view, however, continued to be conservative.[10]

In 1893, a Lutheran professor at Muhlenberg College in Allentown, Pennsylvania, noted with insight beyond his time that "a workingman's needs, his decencies, his luxuries, are no inconsiderable sum: reduce his earnings below that, and he is dissatisfied; but likewise is he clamorous for more." There seemed, however, "no way out of this tangle" except to leave the matter "just where it is now," because "demand and supply must regulate it."[11]

In the 1890s, however, opinions were increasingly voiced, both from within the churches and without, that Christians could no longer leave the state of society "just where it is now," and that the church had a responsibility to participate in social and economic reform. To this the beleaguered churches were quick to answer that the need of the world was regeneration, not reformation. Even progressive Protestants concluded that "the only solution" to the "Labor Question" would be found in "the general diffusion of Christian duty on the part of employer and employed."[12]

In 1892 the Episcopalian *Churchman* complained that labor demanded from the church "unqualified partisanship, . . . a preemptory decision and public assertion that, in every dispute, the employers and the capitalists are on the wrong side." This journal declared that churches "have no commission to do anything of the kind," since "no class of human beings is always . . . right." The *Churchman* stoutly asserted that if workingmen were alienated from the churches because the clergy refused to be "judges and dividers" beyond their province, then "in that case workingmen must remain alienated."[13]

In the 1880s and the 1890s, strikes became widespread—from the Pittsburgh strike in 1877 to the Haymarket Affair in 1886 to the frightening Pullman strike of 1893. The accompanying riots and death and destruction only strengthened the churches in their ambivalent and judgmental attitude toward labor. Labor seemed no longer a slave, already a voter and politician, and well on the way to becoming a tyrant. Some Protestants claimed that Chrisitianity had been, and continued to be "labor's best friend." But the burning resentment of labor toward the churches, with their patronizing, condescending attitude and their aggressive proselytization, continued to smoulder. The chasm between church and labor gradually widened—until, to Protestants, the Labor Question seemed equivalent to, or even synonymous with, the larger Social Question that continued to vex and puzzle America as a nation: the question of whether, and how, a heterogeneous society might endure.[14]

The Social Question, in fact, became so integral to the thinking of Americans in general that, although philosophers, sociologists, and economists pondered upon it constantly, few thought it necessary to spell out the question, or to define and describe it. Those who did try despaired of definition, but everyone seemed to come to some common undefined consensus as to the real existence and complex substance of the Social Question. "But who can say just what it is in particular?" asked one. "The doctors differ as to the disease."

"Doctors" of many sorts were to differ as to the disease and the cure for many years, but during those years many foretold and marked the growing chasm between capital and labor. For Protestants, "the great social question of our day and land, . . . of all days and all lands," was a labor problem: "What work shall have white bread, and what shall have brown, and how much of either shall it be?"[15]

In 1889 a Canadian, viewing the problem from abroad, warned that "labor and capital . . . are gradually drawing off into separate camps" and concluded that the only possible "practical outcome" would be "a condition of hostility." In 1897 Baptist institutional church pastor Edward Judson sadly noted that "a new patch shrinks on an old garment, so that the rent is made worse. The more perfectly workingmen are organized, the wider will be the chasm between them and their employers."[16]

In 1904, Charles W. Eliot, president of Harvard University, was to report that "capital and labor are growing farther away from one another day by day, and I can foresee no settlement except the shedding of blood." In 1905, John R. Commons, by then at the University of Wisconsin, was to add his voice in a renewed warning that "no question more difficult could be assigned" than the one of "the relationship between ethics and the modern competitive system." In 1908 he was to write a lengthy treatise on the question, "Is Class Conflict in America Growing and Is it Inevitable?"[17]

The question did, in fact, appear to be inevitable. Looking back in retrospect on the respective positions of church and labor in the 1890s, however, it would seem that labor created the chasm that separated it from the church and that the churches accepted it, almost reluctantly. At the University Settlement on Forsyth Street in New York City, for example, it was discovered that "creators of public opinion among the working people deprecate everything that tends to conciliate the factions," and that workingmen "of the extremer class" said they could accomplish far more for their cause "by intensifying class feeling" and by teaching that "half-way measures were palliative, worse than useless in the long run." In spite of this adamant stand on the part of labor, however, the Protestant churches patiently sought solutions to the Social Question—but without compromising their evangelistic goals.[18]

COOPERATIVE EVANGELISM

In the early 1890s a few calm, farseeing Protestant leaders, most of them in the institutional church movement, began to plead with the churches to soften their hardened judgments of labor, to take a rational look at the problems of labor, and to hunt for intelligent new approaches to their solution. In 1891, William Jewett Tucker, president of Dartmouth College, called upon the Christian church to "admit the rights of agitation and of organization" and asked for "clear and sufficient recognition" of the labor movement—"not the indorsement of all its methods, . . . but the honorable recognition of the principle . . . and of the human beings it represents." From the settlements, Robert A. Woods of the Andover House in Boston asked ministers to give up "the unknown tongue of conventional culture and religion" and learn the language of the workingman, who "must be met upon the basis of his convictions whether he is the victim of prejudice or not." By the late 1890s a number of Protestant clergymen had reached the understanding that the labor problem was "not a question of mere justice" but rather "the question of a complete and satisfied manhood, . . . a cry for the recognition of the essential *manhood* of every true worker in every sphere of life."[19]

University of Chicago sociologist Charles Richmond Henderson was, perhaps, foremost among those pleading for reform movements to become "more positive and really ministrant." He noted that workingmen had carried with them from the churches to the friendly societies and labor lodges a Christian ritual and the affectionate salutation "brother," which had become unfashionable in the church. He urged "educated Christian men" to seek friends and converts in these "chosen retreats of men wounded at heart, misled by prejudice, hurt at real or fancied slights, and alienated from the communion and duties of the body of Christ." He listed community needs, such as relief of the poor, that could not be met by "isolated action" and urged the churches in each community to "make treaties with democracy in order to bless the movement and mingle its leaven with the aspirations of the modern rulers of society." Insisting that Christ "had in mind some kind of league," he consistently emphasized "the need of co-operation of all churches with each other, and with allied agencies."[20]

The institutional church movement was indeed accompanied by a concurrent and widespread effort to bring together the multitudinous, fragmented sects and denominations of American Protestantism, especially for the purposes of practical work and united reform effort. "There is a sound of a 'going in the tops of the mulberry trees,' a stirring of the air," the *Presbyterian* had exulted in 1887. "Christians of all denominations are drawing together in ways unheard-of before; they are meeting for prayer and conference."[21]

Theological seminary students were among the first to make an active move toward cooperation. In 1879 theological students at Princeton had expressed a desire for "some co-operation," and the autumn of the following year saw the first annual convention of the American Inter-Seminary Missionary Alliance, representing twelve seminaries. At the first convention, papers were read by the Reverend H.M. Scudder of Brooklyn and the Reverend Edward Judson, then of Orange, New Jersey.[22]

The 1880s brought a great many conferences and associations formed for the purpose of cooperative evangelistic effort. In part, this trend was occasioned by "the abrasion of mind with mind, the battle of ideas, the content of sentiments, as between Christianity and various forms of unbelief." Protestant leaders were also increasingly embarrassed by the absurdity of "planting a half-dozen rival churches in a small frontier village scarcely large enough to afford a congregation for one," while "hundreds and thousands of non-churchgoing people" were congregating in large cities.[23]

In 1884 an interdenominational congress was held in Cincinnati to consider the problems of city evangelism, and the American Congress of Churches held its first meeting in Hartford, with "a good portrait" of the "dear old Dr. Bushnell" in "a conspicuous position." The second meeting of the Congress was held in Cleveland in 1886. There was a discussion of "The Workingman's Distrust of the Church: Its Causes and Remedies," and Rainsford argued for "readjustments in our methods of dealing with and reaching the poor." In the same year the "Two Sams," Georgia evangelist Sam Jones and his disciple Sam Small, were bringing together "the most interesting audiences" in church union efforts in Chicago and Baltimore. In Chicago it was reported that the audiences were "neither of the highest nor of the lowest people in the social scale, but of the great middle class that do Chicago's work." A committee of seventeen denominations was formed for city evangelism in Pittsburgh; in Philadelphia three hundred churches joined in a plan to visit every house in the city. In 1887 a Philadelphia Evangelistic Union was proposed, as a permanent organization for "general and systematic visitation of families."[24]

In New York City, in the 1890s, Rainsford was instrumental in bringing together various churches and settlements to form a Federation of East Side Workers, resulting in various forms of useful cooperation. The Federation established a committee of lawyers, to constitute a Bureau of Justice that would maintain the legal rights of the poor "against the oppression of landlords, employers, and tradesmen," and appointed another committee to enforce the sanitary laws. Another influential group—the Industrial Christian Alliance—worked with the Children's Aid Society, the King's Daughters, the Roman Catholic St. Vincent de Paul Society, and the public schools to help the poor and the unemployed and to combat saloons by operating seven restaurants where, for five cents, a "substantial meal" could be "eaten on the premises or carried home."[25]

MOVEMENT TOWARD FEDERATION

Cooperative reform activities were, in fact, bringing the churches closer to federation on a national scale. Various denominational "Social Unions" took the lead in moving toward federation. In 1894 in New York over a thousand people were present when the Baptist, Methodist, and Presbyterian Social Unions and the Congregational Club met "to talk and eat together." In 1897 the Christian League of Philadelphia, which had been suggested by the Presbyterian Social Union in 1894, was founded for the promotion of "moral purity, temperance, Sabbath observance," and for cooperation with other societies to improve the conditions of "the neglected, ignorant, unprotected, and debased." Organized "for business, not for play," the League tore down old condemned buildings in the slums and carried on a mission and school in the center of "Chinatown." All of the volunteer teachers were men, for it was "not deemed wise" to have women teachers.[26]

In 1895 over twenty-five hundred delegates, mainly "directly engaged in hand-to-hand, practical work among the masses," gathered in New Haven in the ninth annual convention of the International Christian Workers' Association to hear such speakers as Baptist preacher Russell Conwell and Newman Smyth, pastor of New Haven's Center Church. The convention discussed such subjects as institutional churches, social settlements, good government clubs, boys' work, and work among "prisoners and fallen women," as well as "soldiers, sailors, police, miners, lumbermen, steerage passengers, and railroad men."[27]

It was reported that in New York City cooperative Christian work "had a most ephemeral and disheartening history," but even there a Federation of Churches and Christian Workers was successfully established in 1895 and began significant work. This group was formed in response to a pamphlet issued by the Reverend J. Winthrop

Hegeman, pastor of Christ Episcopal Church, Riverdale. After discarding several methods of house-to-house canvassing, the Federation supplied all the materials and bore the entire expense of tabulating and reporting a house-to-house canvass of the Fifteenth Assembly District. In the winter of 1896 it collected "social and religious statistics" concerning over eight thousand families and recommended the establishment of a Protestant Episcopal church, a Lutheran church, industrial schools, circulating libraries, and kindergartens. This cooperative effort resulted in a sub-federation called Auxiliary "A," which included all churches within the area, the YMCA, the YWCA Settlement on West Forty-seventh Street, and Hartley House, the industrial settlement of the Association for Improving the Condition of the Poor. Leighton Williams, pastor of Amity Baptist Church, served as president of the Auxiliary.[28]

The Federation of Churches and Christian Workers in New York was headed by two men who became prominent in the growing national movement for church federation—the Reverend Frank Mason North, president of the council of the Federation, and the Reverend Walter Laidlaw, executive secretary of the Federation. A second house-to-house canvass was completed in 1898. Cooperative parishes were formed to reach twenty-three thousand families in the Fifteenth and Seventeenth Assembly Districts. A "large wall calendar" was distributed to every family, with "full information about the churches, day schools, evening schools, high schools, industrial schools, Bible workers' schools, libraries, museums, clubs, savings banks, baths, dispensaries, etc., etc., of the entire territory, and, for the benefit both of landlord and tenant, the tenement-house law." The Federation also helped to enforce the public school law.[29]

PROTESTANT SETTLEMENTS

It was in regard to ministry to neighborhoods that institutional church philosophy and social settlement philosophy found their point of intersection. University of Chicago theologian Shailer Mathews wrote that the "social task" of the church was to be "an institution of its neighborhood." Edward Judson described the institutional church as "the local church girdled with philanthropic institutions, each on a small scale, meeting the needs of the neighborhood—an orphanage, dispensary, hospital, home for the aged and so on." Walter Laidlaw, New York leader in church federation, called upon the churches to provide "an abiding ministry to neighborhoods that need it." Charles Stelzle considered his Hope Chapel in Minneapolis to be "in every sense" a social settlement, "although never known by that name."[30]

Some of the early settlements in America, in fact, were established under distinct Protestant auspices with Protestant leadership. Several years before 1887, when Stanton Colt began the work on Forsythe Street that is generally credited as the historical beginning of settlement house work in America, the Reverend James O.S. Huntington "took residence in lower New York, in a similar manner" and "lived and labored effectively, . . . gathering the working people around him in religious and social and club life." At that time Huntington succeeded the Reverend Henry C. Potter as rector of Grace Episcopal Church, which, with each year, became "a more pronounced influence in the densely peopled region from Fourteenth Street to Tenth, east of Fourth Avenue." In 1896 the old chapel was "secularized" under William Reed Huntington and George R. Bottome to include the House of Anna for aged women, the House of Simeon for aged men, the House of the Holy Child for dependent children, a kindergarten and day nursery, apartments for the clergy and deaconesses, and "ample provision for club work of every kind." In 1897 it was reported that "the presence of fifteen active residents, eight men and seven women, all engaged in the most earnest social and humanitarian work upon avowedly Christian principles, gives this institution undisputed settlement standing.''[31]

One of the most active Protestant settlements was East Side House, at the foot of East Seventy-sixth Street in New York City, carried on through individual contributions and funds provided by the Episcopalian Church Club of New York. Episcopalian bishop Henry C. Potter, sociologist Franklin H. Giddings, and J. Pierpont Morgan were vice-presidents of the House. It opened in 1891 with residents who were graduates of Harvard, Trinity, Bowdoin, and Cornell. It also had a close connection with Columbia College. Its major activities were a men's social club called the East Side Club, with a membership of 160, and the Webster Free Library of 4,000 volumes.[32]

In Chicago, All Souls Church opened the Helen Heath Settlement after the 1893 depression, and the Seventh Day Adventist Medical Missionary and Benevolent Association sponsored a Medical Missionary College Settlement. In 1894 the Congregational churches of St. Paul established St. Paul Commons, "the first settlement organized on a business basis and made self-sustaining from the beginning," with a lodging house, woodyard, labor exchange, library, educational league, and gymnasium. Other Christian settlements included the Berean Social Settlement, the first in Detroit, avowedly Christian and "in many senses a mission," with emphasis upon "social purity" and "the problem of homemaking"; Christodora House, in a Chicago locality "crowded with evil resorts," calling itself "evangelical non-ecclesiastical, educational yet devout, humanitarian without ignoring Christ," and the Willard "Y" House in Boston, under the auspices of the Young Women's Christian Temperance Union of Massachusetts.[33]

Protestant leaders came to embrace the settlement as the only way to evangelize "the densely populated places," where "poverty, ignorance, and vice are concentrated." Frank Mason North, an editor of *Open Church,* believed that the Great Physician belonged in dispensaries and the Christ of Nazareth in carpenter shops. He called it "needless timidity" for social settlements to "have excluded the definite confession of Christ as the essence of their motive." He called for "Mission Homes" insteasd of "Mission Halls" and declared that "wherever a church is central to a great population, it should include a Gospel Settlement."[34]

AGGRESSIVE CAMPAIGNS

Urban clergymen interested in urban welfare and reform came to realize that their efforts were greatly hampered and often nullified by the machine system of political bossism in American cities; so it was in the area of municipal reform that Protestant churches chose to concentrate their aggressive efforts in the 1890s. Scattered Protestant municipal reform activity already had begun in the 1880s in the form of "Sabbath Leagues" and "Law and Order Leagues" aimed at obtaining from city and state governments more efficient enforcement of existing laws pertaining to Sunday, to vice, and to public order. A Sabbath League existed in New Orleans as early as 1882, and a Law and Order League was founded in New Jersey in 1887 "to enforce the laws of the State of New Jersey so far as they relate to public order." In the 1890s these groups became quite aggressive, widening the sphere of their activity, and many new Protestant reform groups appeared. "It seems to have fallen to the ministers, especially to those holding prominent pulpits, to 'prod' the police of our cities to a more vigilant and faithful performance of their duties," reported the *Presbyterian* in 1894.[35]

In New Haven, for example, Newman Smyth, president of the Law and Order League of that city, confronted the police commissioners "with earnest demands that the laws against evil resorts, and open temptation to vice be enforced," stirring the police to "unusual efforts." In 1893 the Pilgrim Association, composed of representatives of the Congregational churches of Boston, was formed to seek the cooperation of the religious and philanthropic clubs of the city in considering the "best methods" of municipal government and to bring "those who neglect their civic duties" to realize their respon- sibilities. This movement differed from its predecessors in that it did not propose to form a new citizens' organization, but rather made use of those already in existence.[36]

One of the most active and influential reform groups was the City Vigilance League of New York City, also founded in 1893. Its secretary was William Howe Tolman, executive officer of the Association for the Improvement of the Poor, and its president was the Reverend Charles H. Parkhurst, who was to become the most colorful and controversial figure in the Protestant campaign for municipal reform. The sole object of the organiza- tion was to promote "whatever makes for good citizenship" by work in assembly and election districts and study of practical phases of city life.[37]

"Vigilance implies watchfulness and watchfulness elicits the facts," explained Tolman. The League based its work on that of Charles Booth in London. Four hundred "hand-picked" men situated in districts "all over the city" studied and investigated such questions as the problems of sanitation, the abuses of the "sweating" system, and popular amusements. Like the Congregational movement in Boston, this group cooperated with other reform groups, such as the Committee of Seventy, headed by Joseph Larocque; the New York Civil Service Reform Association, headed by Seth Low, and Parkhurst's well-known Society for the Prevention of Crime. All of these groups worked in opposition to Tammany rule in New York.[38]

The City Vigilance League of New York became the model for other groups around the country, such as the Civic Federation of Chicago (1894), the Christian Citizen's League of Chicago (1896), and vigilance committees in San Francisco and Sacramento. The Civic Federation of Chicago, for example, carried on a vigorous war against gam- bling, as reported in the *Presbyterian,* 10 October 1894:

> Chicago is just now greatly stirred by the facts in regard to gambling, brought to light by the Civic Federation. The Committee on Morals, under the leadership of the Rev. W.G. Clarke, pastor of the Campbell Park Presbyterian Church, has quietly gone forward securing evidence, and the time having come, one or two effective blows were struck . . . through the county sheriff. Notorious places were raided, and the paraphernalia of the gamblers was taken into the streets and smashed into kindling wood. . . . The tremendous mass meetings on Sabbath afternoon gave expression to the public indignation, and the Mayor promised to enforce the law.[39]

In 1894, *Aggressive Methodism,* a monthly devoted to city evangelization, extolled the "wonderful results" that may be accomplished by volunteer effort and claimed that "the present Board of Health and the present Street Cleaning Department" in New York City were both established as a result of citizens' movements "not notable for numerical strength." In 1895 the *Independent* reported that attention had also been called to "the shortcomings of municipal administration" in New Orleans, Cincinnati, Philadelphia, and other cities.[40]

As they had done with the institutional church, Protestant clergymen and laymen looked upon their reform efforts as an expression of Christian duty and Christian stewardship, and as a means of evangelism. Conventions and mass meetings held in the interest of municipal reform came to be called "open doors for the Gospel"; and it was claimed that spiritual life "would be abundantly protected and fostered, if only the ideals of righteousness, which are embodied in the Gospel, might find some practical expression in the laws of municipal life." It was suggested that "every Christian worker should be a specialist in the treatment of the woes of men" and that reforming the abuses of society was "missionary service."[41]

In 1894 a national conference for the promotion of Christian principles in civil government was held in Washington, and in 1898 a Protestant pastor wrote in the *Christian City* that the downtown preacher should be a leader in "all civic affairs," and that the "supreme interest" of the downtown church should be "every social necessity, such as better tenements, pure water, clean streets, small parks, improved drainage, oversight of child life." John R. Commons named "the right heart and the right social reform" as "the two prime methods of the kingdom of heaven." He claimed that since "governments are ordained by God," then "God surely is pretty vitally connected with . . . politics," and that therefore "to register a clean Christian ballot for honest men upon election day is a sacred duty."[42]

This Protestant philosophy of social reform was epitomized in the personality and the aggressive activity of Charles H. Parkhurst, called the "fearless" and "clear-voiced" herald of organized warfare upon corruption in municipal government. Trained at a country college in Massachusetts, and passing from the pastorate of a Massachusetts country church to one of the most prominent pulpits in New York, Parkhurst "proved himself not only the herald of war, but the heroic protagonist and the consummate leader when the battle is hottest and the struggle most deadly and decisive."[43]

Hinting the "suspicion" that parishioners of his new appointment, the Madison Square Presbyterian Church in New York, "would rather see the poor people of lower New York in hell than coming into their pews on Sunday, cluttering them up with their old clothes," Parkhurst brought twenty families of his congregation "in some measure into touch with twenty other families on the East Side." He insisted that "professionally insulated" clergymen must learn the vernacular of the unconverted, and also persuaded his congregation to take the Church of Sea and Land as a mission for a year, teaching that "the best things that God makes are the ones that show most capacity to adjust themselves to altered environment.[44]

Parkhurst soon discovered that "the problem of converting an American city to Jesus Christ is a long and complicated one." He set about his task with unprecedented sweep and fury. Upon the death of the Reverend Howard Crosby he became president of the Society for the Prevention of Crime. It was reported that "even rummy justices, saloon grand jurors, and unspeakable police captains" had been awed by the strong personality of Crosby. Now the lawbreakers "breathed more easily for a while," expecting Parkhurst to "take it out in rhetoric and preaching, or in bustling around for a little," since he was literary, country bred, and inexperienced.[45]

Parkhurst's intensive efforts, however, made him more feared than Crosby had ever been. He decided on a frontal all-out attack on the Tammany organization, which he said "fosters the tendency to crime," and proceeded to shake Tammany Hall to its foundations. It had been soundly trounced once before, twenty years earlier, when boss William Marcy Tweed had been convicted "for stealing from the city, as well as forgery and conspiracy."[46]

Parkhurst, in making his foolhardy decision, followed in the footsteps of a vigorous precursor—the popular Presbyterian preacher Thomas DeWitt Talmage, whose sermons were at one time carried by thirty-five hundred newspapers. It was reported that when Talmage preached in his Brooklyn Tabernacle, as he reached the climax of his discourse, the platform seemed "to present a whirling and kaleidoscopic view of legs and arms," and that he closed with "a grand pyrotechnical peroration, composed partly of hand-springs and partly of hallelujahs."

In 1878, Talmage's sermons became descriptions of "his travels by night through the evil places of New York," in which he was escorted by two elders of his congregation and two stout, armed policemen. Claiming that "we need fifty Comstocks," Talmage reported that judges, church officers, stockbrokers, wholesale grocers, and merchants patronized the houses of ill fame. "I could call names," shrieked Talmage, "and I may before I get through, though it wreck the fabric of society."

The New York *Times* answered Talmage in lively rebuttal. The *Times* insisted that Talmage didn't even get out of his carriage on his nightly escapades, and that the "phenomenal gambling-house" that Talmage claimed to have visited "exists principally in his mind." The *Times* concluded that Talmage was "as loose in his tongue as he is in the joints," and called him a "charlatan" and a "slanderer"—a man "doing his level best to bring into disrepute the sacred cause which he professes to serve."[47]

Neither Tweed's earlier conviction nor Talmage's perorations did much damage to Tammany Hall. By 1892, Tammany had been restored to "all its power and prosperity" by Richard Croker, chairman of its finance committee and the power behind the "hack" Democratic mayor, Hugh J. Grant. On 14 February 1892, Parkhurst, in a regular Sunday morning sermon in his church, plunged into a "blistering attack" on the New York municipal administration, and called Tammany Hall "a lying, perjured, rum-soaked, and libidinous lot." In particular, he accused the New York police department of sharing the earnings of prostitutes and racketeers, and of receiving bribes from "thousands" of saloon-keepers in return for illegal permission to keep their establishments open on Sunday. "While we try to convert criminals, they manufacture them!" was his cry.

The next day much of the text of Parkhurst's sermon appeared in the New York *World,* and nine days later he was called before the grand jury of the Court of General Sessions and asked to produce "solid evidence of police corruption." Unfortunately, Parkhurst had no documented evidence to offer, and the grand jury rebuked him for "instilling in the citizens of New York an unwarranted feeling of distrust toward their officials." Humiliated by his experience, Parkhurst determined to obtain first-hand experience of New York night life in the slums. Drawing on the previous experience and private advice of Talmage, Parkhurst enlisted the assistance of David J. Whitney, one of the founders of the Society for the Prevention of Crime, and John Langdon "Sunbeam" Erving, one of his parishioners. The three of them, having concocted elaborate disguises, embarked on a legendary tour of saloons, lodging houses for derelicts, and "complete colonies of houses of prostitution."

In March the trio visited "a luxurious brothel run by Mrs. Hattie Adams, at 31 and 33 East Twenty-seventh Street." Soon after that, Mrs. Adams was sued by her landlord for violating her lease by running a "disorderly" house. Parkhurst was called to testify at her trial. Mrs. Adam's lawyers, the notorious Howe and Hummel, were certain that a staid, literary, conservative Protestant clergyman like Parkhurst would never admit in a court of law that he had visited and played "leapfrog" in a brothel. They were mistaken, and from then on Parkhurst was front-page news and the acknowledged catalyst for Protestant municipal reform efforts in a number of cities.

Parkhurst's escapades yielded the "solid evidence" that the grand jury had requested. He presented "affadavits from private detectives proving that on Sunday, March 6th, at least 254 Manhattan saloons had served at least 2,438 drinkers, including a good many policemen." Parkhurst was thus able to close "a majority of the saloons" on Sundays. Even more important, he stimulated the grand jury to bring in a remarkable unanimous presentment directly accusing the police department of protecting vicious places. The grand jury also sent a protest to the state legislature opposing the Spies Bill, which would make it difficult to secure evidence against disorderly places. The *Independent* rallied to Parkhurst's support and called him the "apostle of a purer era," asserting that he had "voiced, developed, and concentrated" public opinion and urging the citizens of New York to stand behind him and his Society for the Prevention of Crime.

In 1893 many civic organizations and newspapers in New York began to join Parkhurst in a "clamor" for a state investigation of municipal corruption. The Democratic administration of Governor Roswell P. Flower paid no attention to them, but the November elections created Republican majorities in the legislature, which in January 1894 appointed the famous Lexow Committee, headed by state senator Clarence E. Lexow, which "exposed police corruption in New York more thoroughly than it had ever been exposed before, or has been ever since."[48]

In 1894, Parkhurst organized the Woman's Municipal League of New York City "to overcome Tammany control," and also realized a "wonderful redemption of New York City" by organizing the "best elements" of the city to elect a mayor and other officials who were in sympathy with proposed and needed municipal reforms. Following this victory, New York dailies that had long regarded Parkhurst as a "crank" began to praise him highly. Christian leaders suddenly rushed to his support, calling him a "protestant Savonarola" of "noble spirit and dauntless courage." In the spring of 1894 the *Presbyterian* had accused Parkhurst of having in mind "nothing but the negative task of defeating Tammany" and of "lacking in constructive programmes and in progressive municipal ideals." After the fall elections, however, the *Presbyterian* asserted that the investigations of the Lexow Committee had made it evident that "wickedness in high places, sending its contagion down to the lowest officials . . . must, if possible, be brought to a perpetual end," and that "as respects human agency," great credit must be given to the "courageous and persistent" Charles H. Parkhurst for revealing this truth to American Protestants.[49]

Even conservative Protestant denominations had high praise for him. Henry C. Potter, the Episcopalian bishop of New York, in an address at the centennial commencement exercises of Union University, described him as "that clear and vigorous and acute mind" that might yet light the "black fires" that could burn up the "rubbish" of bossism throughout the commonwealth. A Lutheran writer called him "first and foremost a lover of men," and thus "invincible in his fight for probity and decency in the administration of public trusts." In 1897 a Protestant layman wrote that "when a bold champion of the right, like Dr. Parkhurst, attacks single-handed the corruptions of a great city, he is transcending not one jot or tittle the legitimate functions of the church which is pledged to promote the principles of Christ's kingdom."[50]

"When Dr. Parkhurst becomes slashing, he always becomes discourteous and untrue," the *Presbyterian* had noted in the spring of 1894. Parkhurst, however, mellowed considerably in later years, as can be sensed in his sermon to the Thirtieth National Conference of Charities and Correction in 1903:

It takes a great deal of humaneness to deal with humans. . . . We never accomplish constructive results . . . save as our efforts are strung upon a thread of intention that is affectionate and sympathetic. . . .

[Christ] would never had advertised gospel services for the 'masses.' The word is not a gospel word. . . . The Angels, we are told, rejoice over one sinner that repententh, rejoice over them, that is, sinner by sinner. . . .

This quiet man-by-man mode of procedure . . . has to do with what we rather ambitiously call 'settling the questions' that confront us in all this range of humanitarian endeavor. Rarely if ever do we settle a question. . . . Problems work themselves out and we get the advantage . . . if we are standing by when the performance is going on.[51]

The charisma of Parkhurst remained strong throughout the first decade of the twentieth century. His spirit was behind the League for Social Service, organized in 1899 with Josiah Strong as president and William Howe Tolman as secretary. Its immediate objectives were "industrial betterment and city improvement." Strong joined Phillips Brooks, Henry Drummond, Jenkin Lloyd Jones, and other socially minded Protestant clergymen in the Christian City movement of the early 1900s. Its goal was control of American cities for Christianity, since "the city is to control the nation," and "the city redeemed" is the symbol of "heaven on earth—the kingdom fully come."[52]

In reporting Parkhurst's victories in 1894, the *Presbyterian* had credited "ministers of the Gospel, friends of pure politics, lovers of clean government, defenders of the home and of society" with the "glorious result," and had insisted that "what has been done there, can be done elsewhere." What was done in New York *was* done again elsewhere, in the civic uprising in Philadelphia that swept the Cameron and Quay dynasties out of rule in 1905, by ousting Israel W. Durham, the Quay lieutenant who had bossed the city for seven years.

Under Durham, elections had become a farce in Philadelphia; in the best wards more than half of the citizens refused to vote. In 1898 the Municipal League had been organized to overthrow this "despotic and nefarious rule," called by the *Lutheran Observer* "as unscrupulous and corrupt as Tammany in New York." But then something happened. In 1905 "the pent-up anger of the people, long outraged and despoiled of civil rights, . . . broke loose. The people shouted with one voice and the solid organization walls fell like a house of cards." Mayor John Weaver gathered about him an advisory board, a sort of nonpolitical cabinet, and the city began to move forward to "a higher and better municipal life, one worthy of a free people." *The Congregationalist and Christian World* credited this "remarkable" episode in municipal life to an aroused Christian spirit and cited "letters, resolutions, and petitions" that poured in from individual churches and ministers, as well as "prayer meetings . . . turned into patriotic assemblies."[53]

In 1906 the *Outlook* commented that, although a political boss might seem "unshakable," the truth of the matter was that "any tide of public indignation may sweep away the foundations of his authority in a single day"; and that therefore "the boss and machine systems are doomed," for the reasons that they imply the denial of the right of self-government, the abandonment of political responsibility, and the surrender of public liberties. The *Outlook* pleaded for men in public life who will have "some of the instincts of the statesman," so that Americans will "be able to hold our heads up . . . when we face the rest of the world"—a point of view also held by the *Churchman,* which noted that "Admirals Dewey and Schley have made the machine politician an anachronism" and asserted that "if we are to become a world-power, we must . . . elevate our political life at home."[54]

As the *Outlook* expressed it, "The American people are now demanding three very simple things, and they will secure them": free government—"that is to say, the management of public affairs by the people"; honest government, and "an open field and square deal." This was the spirit and aim of the Progressive movement in America, with which Protestants everywhere closely identified themselves in their reform efforts in the early twentieth century.[55]

DEFINING THE SOCIAL ROLE OF THE CHURCH

In the civic vigilance committees, law and order leagues, and aggressive municipal campaigns, militant Protestants sought to demonstrate that, "in the interest of good city government," the church, instead of allowing itself to be ruled out of politics, should "carry religion into politics and subdue it," and thus make Christian morality "a dominant and controlling factor in all human government." In general, however, institutional church leaders believed that church welfare efforts "ought not to replace State effort, but to be independent of it, and to supplement it."[56]

Graham Taylor saw the welfare role of the church as innovative. In 1899 he spoke of the "function of the churches to initiate social movements and agencies for the realization of the Christian ideal, but not to be their executive." Charles Stelzle saw the church as a coordinator of welfare, a "home and center" about which "great movements of reform and reconstruction" might "organize and unify themselves." Washington Gladden described the welfare role of the church as "one of sympathetic co-operation," having the function of inspiring and interpreting social endeavors.[57]

The Open and Institutional Church League saw the church as filling gaps in welfare or as offering alternatives where cultural mechanisms had failed. It asserted that "where other institutions of the community, especially the home, fail to meet and minister to the wants of people, it is necessary and obligatory upon the churches as far as possible to provide substitutes for them." The League, accordingly, promoted such agencies as kindergartens to make up for deficiencies in the public schools or in family life in the slums.[58]

In 1905 an institutional church pastor in Boston called the church "the laboratory for social experiments, where the principles of Christ are carried out in the world of daily life." He described the church as "useful" as a "maid-of-all-work," to supplement society "on any side which it finds to be lacking." He admitted that an institutional church "had little place in a city which is properly balanced." He declared that "when the home fails to perform her duty, the church must take it up; when the social life of a community is limited or degraded, the church must supply a suitable social life; . . . when the community is ignorant of the common necessities of daily life, of cooking and housework, the church must see that they are educated in these matters."[59]

Even the heartiest urban pastors, however, grew weary of the losing effort to bring about permanent community reform. Walter Rauschenbusch, who labored long and faithfully as the pastor of the Second German Baptist Church of New York, "a tiny, poverty-stricken congregation near the infamous Hell's Kitchen," wrote vividly of experiences that led him to conclude that the "hatred" between employers and employees was "generated by our system." During the great industrial crisis of the 1890s, he wrote later in his influential *Christianity and the Social Crisis,* "one could hear human virtue cracking and crumbling all around." He described unemployment, alcoholism, and petty crime as "only the tangible expression of the decay in the morale of the working people" and the "corresponding decay in the morality of the possessing classes."[60]

As they entered the twentieth century, socially minded Protestant leaders began to make conscious efforts to shift the welfare burden to government and to define a concept of legal welfare rights. Rauschenbusch complained that many a Protestant minister was being forced by social conditions to be "an employment bureau," dealing with "out-of-works." He asserted that ministers had become "the scapegoat of others" and had "a right to object against the way human wreckage is being dumped down on them to cure and set up again." Henderson believed that "philanthropy is carrying a burden which does not belong to it, and at tremendous cost, and that is the burden of industry." He concluded that, where voluntary effort was unsuccessful, the people must appeal to the legal profession, to their congressmen, and to the president of the United States for a "legal, righteous way" to obtain justice. Gladden declared that, if private enterprise and private capital could not find employment for "the multitude who are standing idle in the market-place," then the government should organize for them "employments by which they may eat their own bread, and know that they are getting full measure for what they get, and are not dependent on public or private charity."[61]

In the end, orthodox Social Gospelers heeded the advice of Unitarian democrat Jenkin Lloyd Jones, who in 1900 counseled the church to leave "the hungry stomach and the naked back, the sick child and the poverty-stricken mother" to "the charity of the world." He urged the church to take up "the neglected task of vitalizing spirit, of dealing in ideas, promulgating truths, establishing sympathies." Rauschenbusch maintained that, because of its "failure hitherto," the church had become "fitter to take up its regenerative work." In the first decade of the twentieth century, progressive Protestants came to define the "regenerative work" of American Christianity as the interpretation of God to a secular nation rather than the conversion of an unchurched cosmopolitan nation to fellowship with God within a common Christian community.[62]

The leaders of the "free and open" churches, therefore, turned away from aggressive evangelism and intense reform activity to begin a sustained effort to teach their own denominations about the complex social problems of twentieth century America. They had come to see that mastery of the "enemies"—the nonChristian elements in American urban society—could be achieved only through "patient study" and "judicious preaching of the teachings of Jesus in their significance for the moral interests of modern society." Between 1900 and 1912, most of the larger denominations appointed official social service or social action commissions or agencies, and institutional church leaders were instrumental in bringing into existence in 1908 the Federal Council of the Churches of Christ in America, which continued to articulate welfare concerns of American Protestants.[63]

In its "official phase," orthodox social Christianity "was, again, concerned primarily with the labor problem" and "emphasized the ethical aims of the labor movement, . . . appearing anxious to heal the breach between the churches and the working class." Emphasis was placed upon programs of study about social problems and plans for church and community social action. The view of the social role of the church as providing the "chief sanction" for "moral ideals" found effective articulation and implementation in the 1912 platform of the Commission on the Church and Social Service of the Federal Council of the Churches of Christ.[64]

The influential Commission on the Church and Social Service included many clergymen who had been active in the institutional church movement. Among them were

Frank Mason North, Charles Stelzle, Graham Taylor, Charles L. Thompson, Leighton Williams, Shailer Mathews, Samuel Zane Batten, and Walter Rauschenbusch. Their 1912 platform stated that the Christian church had the "three-fold vocation of conscience, interpreter, and guide of all social movements," serving chiefly "to conserve the gains made in social morality and to sanction certain reforms" that the church could not "directly undertake."[65]

It has been rightly noted that orthodox social Christianity remained essentially a preaching movement—that it accepted "the perfectionist outlook of the evangelistic revivals" and "carried over and translated into social terms the ideal that the Christian community was a fellowship of 'the saved.'" Even the most liberal of the Protestant progressives believed that "only a society of regenerate men can avert cataclysm." Harvard's Francis Greenwood Peabody taught that legislation, organization, arbitration, and cooperation demanded, first of all, the "co-operative man"—the man who could contribute "an endowment of patience, foresight, and fidelity." Rauschenbusch—an extreme liberal among American theologians—advocated "a revolutionary Christianity which will call the world evil and change it" by remolding "all our existing institutions"; yet he insisted that "the fundamental contribution of every man is the change of his own personality."[66]

The Protestant progressives of the late nineteenth century and early twentieth century—like the Puritan Separatists and the "trustees of God" before them—did not achieve their purpose of molding a Christian democracy in America. It is questionable whether they reached even their local or immediate social goals. It has been pointed out by various historians that urban evangelists such as Dwight L. Moody never really communicated with workingmen or the urban poor; that the frantic efforts of Sabbath Leagues brought no permanent civic improvements; that the militant crusades of men such as Charles H. Parkhurst made no permanent dent in the corruption of politics in large cities, and that only a fraction of the Protestant laity took an active part in the social ministry of the free and open churches.[67] It is also true, however, that between 1865 and 1912 the orthodox Social Gospel brought all of the major Protestant denominations in America to a responsible concern for social problems, and for the economic and industrial life of individuals—an emphasis that was to become a significant, enduring, and influential facet of American Protestantism.

NOTES

1. Scudder is quoted in "An Aggressive Church," *Congregationalist,* 5 June 1890.

2. Moseley H. Williams, "New Era of Church Work in Philadelphia," *Open Church* 1 (1897): 61; Emory J. Haynes, "Tremont Temple: A Church in Boston," *Chautauquan* 12 (1890): 51; "New Era of Church Work: Ruggles St. Baptist Church, Boston," *Open Church* 2 (1898): 211; R. Q. Mallard, "Symposium on the Institutional Church. II. Not the Ideal Church," *Homiletic Review* 33 (1897): 88. See "The Hartford Pastors' Mission," *Congregationalist,* 28 Apr. 1887 for Graham Taylor's vivid description of his evangelistic efforts at Fourth Church.

3. The quotations are from Henry C. Bourne, "Four Institutional Churches. I. St. George's, New York," *Congregationalist,* 13 Apr. 1893; Rainsford, "Why Not Endow Our Churches?" *Independent,* 22 May 1894; idem, "East Side Work in This City," *Churchman,* 24 Dec. 1892.

4. " 'The Churches' and Industrial Discontent," *Churchman,* 20 Aug. 1892.

5. "Mr. Stelzle and the Workingmen," *Outlook,* 9 Feb. 1901; and Stelzle, "Institutional Work in a Western Mission," *Open Church* 2 (1898): 358-360. In 1903, Stelzle became superintendent of the Department of Church and Labor of the Board of Home Missions of the Presbyterian Church, of which the stated purpose was "to interpret the church to workingmen and workingmen to the church; to interpret employer and employee to each other." See Charity Organization Department of the Russell Sage Foundation, *Inter-Relation of Social Movements with Information about Sixty-seven Organizations* (New York, 1910).

6. "Report of the Annual Convention of the Open and Institutional Church League," *Open Church* 3 (1899): 22; and "Mr. Stelzle and the Workingmen." See also Charles Stelzle, *Christianity's Storm Center: A Study of the Modern City* (New York, 1907).

7. The quotations are from Huntington, "Some Points in the Labor Question," *Church Review* 48 (1886): 5, 13.

8. The quotations are from Munger, "Lesson of the Strikes. II," *Congregationalist,* 20 June 1872; idem, "Lesson of the Strikes. III," ibid., 27 June 1872; and "Labor or Capital," *Presbyterian,* 3 Oct. 1894.

9. Theodore T. Munger, "Lesson of the Strikes," *Congregationalist,* 13 June 1892.

10. For a detailed presentation of the "new political economy" of Ely, Patten, and others, see Sidney Fine, *Laissez Faire and the General-Welfare State: A Study of Conflict in American Thought, 1865-1901,* Ann Arbor Paperbacks Edition (1964, reprinted from Ann Arbor, 1956), pp. 198-251.

11. M.H. Richards, "Labor: A Revolution and a Problem," *Lutheran Quarterly* 23 (1893): 62, 63.

12. Ibid., 65.

13. " 'The Churches' and Industrial Discontent."

14. See M.H. Richards, "A Penny a Day," *Lutheran Quarterly* 17 (1887): 107.

15. Ibid., 102, 103.

16. Adam Shortt, "Evolution of the Relation between Capital and Labor," *Andover Review* 11 (1889): 145; and Judson, "Symposium on the Institutional Church. VI. The Institutional Church a Remedy for Social Alienation," *Homiletic Review* 33 (1897): 472.

17. Eliot, "Capital and Labor Far Apart," Boston *Evening Transcript,* 16 Jan. 1904; Commons, "Honorable Methods in Business Today," *Congregationalist and Christian World,* 2 Sept. 1905; idem, "Is Class Conflict in America Growing and Is It Inevitable?" *American Journal of Sociology* 13 (1908): 756-783.

18. The quotations are from Morrison I. Swift, "Working Population of Cities and What the Universities Owe Them," *Andover Review* 13 (1890): 599, 600.

19. Tucker, "Authority of the Pulpit in a Time of Critical Research and Social Confusion," *Andover Review* 16 (1891): 397, 398; Woods, "Working Men—One Thing to Say to Them," *Congregationalist,* 9 Mar. 1893; and Edwin Heyl Delk, "Centrality of Christian Fellowship," *Lutheran Quarterly* 25 (1895): 534, 535.

20. Henderson, "Co-operation in Humanitarian Work," *Open Church* 1 (1897): 123, 124. Historian Herbert G. Gutman has supported Henderson's view that Protestantism helped Gilded Age labor leaders to "restore . . . the sense of human solidarity infused with religious values" and has traced a "close relationship between Protestant Nonconformity, especially Methodism, and labor reform." See Gutman, "Protestantism and the American Labor Movement: The Christian Spirit in the Gilded Age," in *The National Temper: Readings in American History,* ed. Lawrence W. Levine and Robert Middlekauff (New York, 1968), pp. 239-248.

21. "The Religious Movement," *Presbyterian,* 8 Jan. 1887.

22. William E. Hull, "The American Inter-Seminary Missionary Alliance," *Lutheran Quarterly* 16 (1886): 549-553.

23. The quotations are from "Church Life and Work: Are They on the Decline?" *Christian Union,* 6 Apr. 1881; and George F. Pentecost, "Evangelization of Our Cities. II," *Homiletic Review* 10 (1885): 396. "Various forms of unbelief" no doubt referred to socialism and anarchism; agnosticism as represented by Robert C. Ingersoll; Unitarianism and Universalism; such transcendental cults as "New Thought"; and, in conservative Protestant circles, even historical criticism within the Christian church.

24. See E.P. Parker, "The American Congress of Religions," *Independent,* 2 May 1884; William Wilberforce Newton, "The Congress of Churches at Cleveland," ibid., 3 June 1886; "The 'Two Sams' in Chicago," ibid., 18 Mar. 1886; J.W. Sproull, "City Evangelization in Pittsburgh," ibid., 20 May 1886; "The Religious Movement," and "Evangelistic Work in Philadelphia Next Winter," *Presbyterian,* 16 July 1887.

25. Rainsford, "East Side Work," and "Charities," *Independent,* 15 Mar. 1894.

26. "Social Unions and Christian Fellowship," *Independent,* 3 Apr. 1894; J.H.W. Stuckenberg, "Social Study and Social Work," *Homiletic Review* 33 (1897): 367; and Moseley H. Williams, "New Era of Church Work in Philadelphia," *Open Church* 1 (1897): 55.

27. "Christian Workers at New Haven," *Congregationalist,* 21 Nov. 1895.

28. The quotations are from Walter Laidlaw, "The Federation of the Churches: What It Is and What It Does," *Christian City* 10 (1898): 388, 389.

29. Ibid., 389-391. See also Thomas Dixon, *Failure of Protestantism in New York and Its Causes* (New York, 1896), pp. 135-147.

30. Mathews, "The Christian Church and Social Unity," *American Journal of Sociology* 5 (1900): 465; Judson, "Symposium on the Institutional Church," 474; Laidlaw, "Christ and the City," *Christian City* 10 (1898): 501; and Stelzle, "Institutional Church in a Western Mission," 360.

31. The quotations are from Swift, "Working Population of Cities," 593fn; Frank Mason North, "New Era of Church Work in the City of New York," *Christian City* 9 (1897): 9, 10; and John Palmer Gavit, ed., *Bibliography of College, Social, and University Settlements* (Cambridge, Mass., 1897), p. 40.

32. *Forward Movements—containing Brief Statements regarding Institutional Churches, Social Settlements, Rescue Missions* (Boston, 1894) pp. 25, 26.

33. All Souls Church, *Twenty-first Annual* (1904), p. 71; Gavit, *Bibliography of College, Social, and University Settlements,* pp. 19, 29-31; and "Christodora House," *Christian City* 12 (1900): 31-33.

34. North, "Church Settlements," *Open Church* 1 (1897): 103.

35. The quotations are from "Reform Needed," *Presbyterian,* 23 July 1887; and "Editorial Items," ibid., 21 Mar. 1894. See also "The Sabbath in New Orleans," *Congregationalist,* 19 Apr. 1882.

36. "A Forward Movement in Government," *Congregationalist,* 16 Mar. 1893; and "Editorial Items," *Presbyterian,* 21 Mar. 1894.

37. Tolman, "Educational Value of Reform Movements," *Congregationalist,* 24 Aug. 1893.

38. Tolman, "Educational Value of Reform Movements," and "News of the Week: Domestics," *Independent,* 9 May 1895. See also William Howe Tolman, *Municipal Reform Movements in the United States: The Textbook of the New Reformation* (New York, 1895), with an introductory chapter by Charles H. Parkhurst. See also Charles Booth, *Life and Labour of the People in London* (London, 1904). Booth's monumental seventeen-volume work was the first "scientific" comprehensive community survey, a method widely copied in the United States and promoted by the Russell Sage Foundation.

39. Melville E. Stone, "The Higher Life of Chicago," *Outlook,* 22 Feb. 1896; "An Era of Municipal Reform," *Independent,* 17 Jan. 1895; and "Correspondence: Chicago," *Presbyterian,* 10 Oct. 1894, from which the quotation is taken.

40. Charles F. Wingate, "How to Make New York a Better City," *Aggressive Methodism,* Mar. 1894; and "An Era of Municipal Reform." See also R. Heber Newton, "The People's Movement for Municipal Reform," *Independent,* 7 Aug. 1890.

41. "The Month," *Aggressive Methodism,* Dec. 1894; "The Month," ibid., Oct. 1894. In 1894 *Aggressive Methodism* became the *Christian City.*

42. "Religious Notes," *Independent,* 24 Apr. 1894; Levi Gilbert, "The Down-Town Church Again," *Christian City* 10 (1898): 382, 383; and Commons, "Social Economics and City Evangelization," *Christian City* 10 (1898): 771, 773.

43. Merrill E. Gates, "Municipal Reform and Tenement Houses," *Independent,* 10 Jan. 1895.

44. Swift, "Working Population of Cities," 601; and Charles H. Parkhurst, "Lay Ministry in New York," *Independent,* 9 Jan. 1890. See also A.E. Dunning, "Expansion of the Local Church," *Andover Review* 17 (1892): 19; and "The Church Forsaking the Common People," *Independent,* 14 Mar. 1895.

45. Parkhurst, "Lay Ministry," and C.S. Harrower, "The Police or the People—Which?" *Aggressive Methodism,* Feb. 1894.

46. The quotations are from "Dr. Parkhurst's Crusade," *Independent,* 17 Mar. 1892; and Morris Robert Werner, *It Happened in New York* (New York, 1957), p. 36.

47. The quotations are from "Talmage's Experiences," New York *Times,* 21 Oct. 1878; "The Specific Sins I Saw," ibid., 28 Oct. 1878; "Rev. Mr. Talmage Out Late," ibid., 18 Nov. 1878; "Talmage Among Thieves," ibid., 25 Nov. 1878; and "Truthful Talmage," ibid., 9 Dec. 1878. See also Talmage, *Social Dynamite: Or, The Wickedness of Modern Society* (Chicago, 1888).

48. This account of Parkhurst's escapades is taken from Werner, *It Happened in New York,* pp. 36-59 and "Dr. Parkhurst's Victory," *Independent,* 7 Apr. 1892. See also Lloyd R. Morris, *Incredible New York: High Life and Low Life of the Last Hundred Years* (New York, 1951). For an entertaining historical account of Howe & Hummel, see Richard H. Rovers, *The Magnificent Shysters: The True and Scandalous History of Howe & Hummel* (New York, 1947).

49. "New York: Municipal Changes," *Presbyterian,* 14 Nov. 1894; George Willis Cooke, "The Institutional Church," *New England Magazine* 14 (1896): 645; and Albert Shaw, "The Higher Life of New York City," *Outlook,* 25 Jan. 1896. See also Parkhurst, *Our Fight with Tammany* (New York, 1895) and Parkhurst's series of articles "To the Women of America" in the 1895 issues of the *Ladies' Home Journal.*

50. "Dr. Parkhurst an Example," New York *Christian Advocate,* 4 July 1895; Delk, "Centrality of Christian Fellowship," 536; and John H. Converse, "From a Layman's Standpoint," *Christian City* 9 (1897): 40, 41.

51. Editorial comment in the *Presbyterian,* 25 May 1894; and Charles H. Parkhurst, "The Betterment of Man," *Proceedings of the Thirtieth National Conference of Charities and Correction* (1903), pp. 18, 19 (hereafter cited as *Proceedings*). See also Parkhurst, "The Stuff that Makes Young Manhood," *Ladies' Home Journal,* Feb. 1896.

52. The quotations are from "Side Lights," *Christian City* 11 (1899): 115; and "Methodism and the Metropolis," *Christian City* 15 (1903): 21.

53. Editorial comment in the *Presbyterian,* 14 Nov. 1894; "Municipal Reform," *Lutheran Observer,* 14 Jan. 1898; and Charles L. Kloss, "Civic Uprising in Philadelphia," *Congregationalist and Christian World,* 1 July 1905.

54. "The Doom of Political Autocracy," *Outlook,* 13 Jan. 1906; and "New Standards of Public Life." *Churchman,* 3 Sept. 1898.

55. "The Doom of Political Autocracy." See also Charles Zueblin, *American Municipal Progress: Chapters in Municipal Sociology* (New York, 1902). For a careful critical appraisal of the Progressive movement that presents opposing points of view, see Arthur Mann, ed., *The Progressive Era: Liberal Renaissance or Liberal Failure* (New York, 1963).

56. The quotations are from E.D. Weigle, "The Ministry and Current Social Problems," *Lutheran Quarterly* 24 (1894): 473; and David Kinley, "Relation of the Church to Social Reform," New York *Christian Advocate,* 7 Sept. 1893.

57. Taylor, "Social Function of the Church," *American Journal of Sociology* 5 (1899): 309; Stelzle, "The Church a Social Force," Louisville *Christian Observer,* 13 Nov. 1912; and Gladden, "The Function of the Church in Social Work: Should It Inspire, Interpret, Guide or Administer It?" *Proceedings* (1911), p. 219.

58. John Bancroft Devins, "For An Open Church: Earnest Work at the Convention of the Institutional League," *Christian City* 11 (1899): 196.

59. John Hopkins Denison, "The Church the Mother of Progress," *Congregationalist and Christian World,* 21 Oct. 1905.

60. Rauschenbusch, *Christianity and the Social Crisis,* Harper Torchbook Edition (1964, edited by Robert D. Cross from New York, 1907), pp. xii., 238. In his Introduction, Cross reported that "several times reprinted, *Christianity and the Social Crisis* eventually sold over 50,000 copies, and was translated into many foreign languages" (Ibid., p. viii). Years later, Harry Emerson Fosdick reported that Rauschenbusch's book "struck home so poignantly on the intelligence and conscience . . . that it ushered in a new era in Christian thought and action" (Benson Y. Landis, ed., *A Rauschenbusch Reader* [New York, 1957], p. xxi).

61. Walter Rauschenbusch, "Stake of the Church in the Social Movement," *American Journal of Sociology* 3 (1897): 26; "Minutes and Discussions," *Proceedings* (1906), p. 599; Washington Gladden, "What to Do with the Workless Man," *Proceedings* (1899), pp. 150, 151.

62. The quotations are from All Souls Church, *Seventeenth Annual* (1900), p. 73; and Rauschenbusch, *Christianity and the Social Crisis,* p. 201.

63. A detailed discussion of the development of social service commissions in Protestant denominations is found in Charles Howard Hopkins, *Rise of the Social Gospel in American Protestantism, 1865-1915* (New Haven, 1940), pp. 280-301, from which the quotations are taken.

64. The quotations are taken from Hopkins, *Rise of the Social Gospel,* pp. 300, 301; and Charles A. Ellwood, "Social Function of Religion," *American Journal of Sociology* 19 (1913): 298-302. See also Samuel Zane Batten, "The Church the Maker of Conscience," *American Journal of Sociology* 7 (1902): 611-628.

65. The quotations are from Allan Hoben, "American Democracy and the Modern Church," *American Journal of Sociology* 21 (1916): 472. The 1912 platform of the Commission on the Church and Social Service is found in Hopkins, *Rise of the Social Gospel,* pp. 316, 317.

66. Paul A. Carter, *Decline and Revival of the Social Gospel: Social and Political Liberalism in American Protestant Churches, 1920-1940* (New York, 1954), pp. 11, 228; M.W. Stryker, "Rights and Duties of Craft and Capital," *Independent,* 2 May 1895; Francis Greenwood Peabody, "Philosophy of the Social Questions," *Andover Review* 8 (1887): 571; and Rauschenbusch, *Christianity and the Social Crisis,* pp. 91, 412.

67. See, for example, William G. McLoughlin, *Modern Revivalism: Charles Grandison Finney to Billy Graham* (New York, 1959), pp. 170, 181; Robert D. Cross in his Introduction to Rauschenbusch, *Christianity and the Social Crisis,* p. ix; Joy J. Jackson, *New Orleans in the Gilded Age: Politics and Urban Progress, 1880-1896* (Baton Rouge, 1969), pp. 90-94; Werner, *It Happened in New York,* p. 116; and Dixon, *Failure of Protestantism,* pp. 77-82.

BIBLIOGRAPHY

The Orthodox Social Gospelers

ABBOTT, LYMAN.
"Sunday Afternoon."
  "The Sunday Question." *Christian Union,* 5 December 1891, pp. 1094-1097.
  "Concerning Worldliness." *Christian Union,* 12 December 1891, p. 1173.
  "The Divinity in Humanity." *Christian Union,* 26 December 1891, p. 1281.
. . . .
  "The Giver of Life." Outlook, 4 March 1893, pp. 424-426.
The Evolution of Christianity. Boston: Houghton, Mifflin & Co., 1892.
"Christ and the Social Order." *Outlook,* 4 January 1896, pp. 23-25.
"Christianity and Democracy." *Outlook,* 11 January 1896, pp. 97-100.
Christianity and Social Problems. Boston: Houghton, Mifflin & Co., 1896.
The Theology of an Evolutionist. Boston: Houghton, Mifflin & Co., 1897.
"Abundant Life." *Outlook,* 9 March 1901, pp. 584-590.
"The Making of a Great Preacher [Phillips Brooks]." *Outlook,* 30 March 1901, pp. 717-720.
The Rights of Man: A Study in Twentieth Century Problems. Boston: Houghton, Mifflin & Co., 1901.
"The Doom of Political Autocracy." *Outlook,* 13 January 1906, pp. 67, 68.
Reminiscences. Boston: Houghton, Mifflin & Co., 1915.

* * *

Brown, Ira Vernon. *Lyman Abbott, Christian Evolutionist: A Study in Religious Liberalism.* Cambridge, Mass.: Harvard University Press, 1953.

COMMONS, JOHN R.
"American Institute of Christian Sociology." *Congregationalist,* 6 July 1893, p. 32.
Social Reform and the Church. With an introduction by Richard T. Ely. New York: T.Y. Crowell & Co., 1894.
"Social Economics and City Evangelization." *Christian City* 10 (1898): 767-772.
"Honorable Methods in Business Today." *Congregationalist and Christian World,* 2 September 1905, p. 311.
"Is Class Conflict in America Growing and Is It Inevitable?" *American Journal of Sociology* 13 (1908): 756-783.
A Documentary History of American Industrial Society. Prepared under the auspices of the American Bureau of Industrial Research, with the co-operation of the Carnegie Institution of Washington. With a preface by Richard T. Ely and an introduction by John Bates Clark. Cleveland: Arthur H. Clark Co., 1910.

ELY, RICHARD T.
"Co-operation in America: In Five Articles."
  I. "Relation of Co-operation to Other Phases of the American Labor Movement." *Congregationalist,* 11 February 1886, p.1.
  II. "Distributive Co-operation." *Congregationalist,* 18 February 1886, p. 2.
  III. "Productive Co-operation." *Congregationalist,* 25 February 1886, p. 2.
  IV. "Other Co-operative Forms." *Congregationalist,* 4 March 1886, p. 2.
  V. "Past Failures and Future Possibilities." *Congregationalist,* 11 March 1886, p. 2.
"Socialism." *Andover Review* 5 (1886): 146-163.
The Labor Movement in America. New York: T.Y. Crowell & Co., 1886.
Social Aspects of Christianity and Other Essays. New York: T.Y. Crowell & Co., 1889.
"The Christian Social Union a Social University." *Churchman,* 26 March 1892, pp. 414, 415.
The Coming City. New York: T.Y. Crowell & Co., 1902.

* * *

Rader, Benjamin G. "Richard T. Ely: Lay Spokesman for the Social Gospel." *Journal of American History* 53 (1966): 61-74.

GLADDEN, WASHINGTON

Working People and Their Employers. Boston: Lockwood, Brooks & Co., 1876.

"The Working People and the Churches." *Independent.* 23 July 1884, pp. 2, 3.

"The Working People and the Churches." *Independent,* 30 July 1884, pp. 4, 5.

"A Plain Talk with Working Men." *Christian Union,* 30 July 1885, p. 8.

Applied Christianity: Moral Aspects of Social Questions. Boston: Houghton, Mifflin & Co., 1886.

"The Perfect Law of Charity." Conference Sermon. *Proceedings of the Twentieth National Conference of Charities and Correction, Chicago, 1893,* pp. 263-278.

Tools and the Man: Property and Industry under the Christian Law. Boston: Houghton, Mifflin & Co., 1893.

"The Church and Social Reform. I." New York *Christian Advocate,* 3 October 1895, p. 635.

"The Church and Social Reform. II." New York *Christian Advocate,* 10 October 1895, p. 652.

"Where Social Reform Should Begin. III." New York *Christian Advocate,* 17 October 1895, pp. 667, 668.

Ruling Ideas of the Present Age. Boston: Houghton, Mifflin & Co., 1895.

Social Facts and Forces: The Factory, the Labor Union, the Corporation, the Railway, the City, the Church. New York: G.P. Putnam's Sons, 1897.

The Christian Pastor and the Working Church. New York: Charles Scribner's Sons, 1898.

"What to Do with the Workless Man." In *Proceedings of the Twenty-sixth National Conference of Charities and Correction, Cincinnati, 1899,* pp. 141-152.

Social Salvation. Boston: Houghton, Mifflin & Co., 1902.

The Church and Modern Life. Boston: Houghton, Mifflin & Co., 1908.

Recollections. Boston: Houghton, Mifflin & Co., 1909.

Being a Christian: What it Means and How to Begin. Boston: The Pilgrim Press, 1910.

The Labor Question. Boston: The Pilgrim Press, 1911.

The School Life. Boston: The Pilgrim Press, 1911.

"The Function of the Church in Social Work: Should It Inspire, Interpret, Guide or Administer It?" Report of the Committee on the Church and Social Work. *Proceedings of the Thirty-eighth National Conference of Charities and Correction, Boston, 1911,* pp. 214-220.

* * *

"Washington Gladden." *Outlook,* 27 January 1906, pp. 154, 155.

The Twenty-fifth Anniversary of the Commencement of the Pastorate of Rev. Washington Gladden over the First Congregational Church of Columbus, Ohio, 1882-1907. Sermon and Addresses. Chicago. Newberry Library. Graham Taylor Collection.

Dorn, Jacob Henry. *Washington Gladden: Prophet of the Social Gospel.* Columbus: Ohio State University Press, 1968.

HENDERSON, CHARLES RICHMOND

"Co-operation of the Churches." In *Proceedings of the Eleventh National Conference of Charities and Correction, St. Louis, 1884,* pp. 80-83.

"Co-operation in Humanitarian Work." *Open Church* 1 (1897): 123-125.

"The Greatest Thing." Abstract of Conference Sermon. *Proceedings of the Twenty-fourth National Conference of Charities and Correction, Toronto, 1897,* pp. 352-354.

"Social Work of Chicago Churches." *Open Church* 2 (1898): 265-270.

"The New Era of Church Work: Immanuel Baptist Church, Chicago." *Open Church* 3 (1899): 10-12.

"The Relation of Philanthropy to Social Order and Progress." President's Address. *Proceedings of the Twenty-sixth National Conference of Charities and Correction, Cincinnati, 1899,* pp. 1-15.

Modern Methods of Charity: An Account of the Systems of Relief, Public and Private, in the Principal Countries Having Modern Methods. New York: The Macmillan Co., 1904.

A Reasonable Social Policy for Christian People. Published for the Social Service Committee of the Northern Baptist Convention. Philadelphia: American Baptist Publication Society, 1909.

Social Duties from the Christian Point of View: A Textbook for the Study of Social Problems. Chicago: University of Chicago Press, 1909.

HODGES, GEORGE

"An Endeavor after Christian Unity." *Independent,* 15 March 1888, pp. 5, 6.

"Religion in the Settlement." In *Proceedings of the Twenty-third National Conference of Charities and Correction, Grand Rapids, 1896,* pp. 150-153.

Faith and Social Service. Eight lectures delivered before the Lowell Institute. New York: Thomas Whittaker, 1896.

"The Progress of Compassion." Conference Sermon. *Proceedings of the Twenty-eighth National Conference of Charities and Correction, Washington, 1901,* pp. 1-11.

The Administration of an Institutional Church: A Detailed Account of the Operation of St. George's Parish in the City of New York. With introductions and comments by President Roosevelt, Bishop Potter and Dr. Rainsford. New York: Harper & Bros., 1906.

Efficient Philanthropy. Extracts from an address delivered at the annual meetings of the associated charities of Columbus, Ohio, and Pittsburgh, Pa. New York: Exchange branch of charity organization societies, 1911.

Everyman's Religion. New York: The Macmillan Co., 1911.

Christianity between Sundays. Revised Edition. New York: The Macmillan Co., 1914.

KING, HENRY CHURCHILL

Reconstruction in Theology. New York: The Macmillan Co., 1901.

Theology and the Social Consciousness: A Study of the Relations of the Social Consciousness to Theology. New York: The Macmillan Co., 1902.

Personal and Ideal Elements in Education. New York: The Macmillan Co., 1902.

Rational Living: Some Practical Inferences from Modern Psychology. New York: The Macmillan Co., 1905.

The Ethics of Jesus. New York: The Macmillan Co., 1910.

The Moral and Religious Challenge of Our Times: The Guiding Principle in Human Development, Reverence for Personality. New York: The Macmillan Co., 1911.

Religion as Life. New York: The Macmillan Co., 1913.

McCULLOCH, OSCAR C.

"The Personal Element in Charity." In *Proceedings of the Twelfth National Conference of Charities and Correction, Washington, 1885,* pp. 340-347.

"The Plymouth Institute." *Christian Union,* 24 December, 1885, p. 25.

* * *

Weeks, Genevieve C. "Religion and Social Work as Exemplified in the Life of Oscar C. McCulloch." *Social Service Review* 39 (1965): 38-52.

_____. "Oscar C. McCulloch: Leader in Organized Charity." *Social Service Review* 39 (1965): 209-221.

MACFARLAND, CHARLES

"The Church and Young Men." *Christian City* 9 (1897): 37-39.

The Spirit Christlike. Boston: The Pilgrim Press, 1904.

The Christian Ministry and the Social Order. Lectures delivered in the course in pastoral functions at Yale Divinity School, 1908/09. New Haven: Yale University Press, 1909.

Spiritual Culture and Social Service. New York: Fleming H. Revell Co., 1912.

Christian Unity at Work. Published by the Federal Council of the Churches of Christ in America, 1913.

Christian Service and the Modern World. New York: Fleming H. Revell Co., 1915.

MATHEWS, SHAILER

The Social Teaching of Jesus: An Essay in Christian Sociology. New York: The Macmillan Co., 1897.

"Significance of the Church to the Social Movement." *American Journal of Sociology* 4 (1899): 603-620.

"The Christian Church and Social Unity." *American Journal of Sociology* 5 (1900): 456-469.

The Gospel and the Modern Man. New York: The Macmillan Co., 1910.

The Social Gospel. Philadelphia: Griffin & Rowland Press, 1910.

The Individual and the Social Gospel. Published jointly by the Missionary Education Movement and Layman's Missionary Movement. New York: Missionary Education Movement of the United States and Canada, 1914.

New Faith for Old: An Autobiography. New York: The Macmillan Co., 1936.

MUNGER, THEODORE T.

"The Lesson of the Strikes." *Congregationalist,* 13 June 1872, p. 1.

"The Lesson of the Strikes. II." *Congregationalist,* 20 June 1872, p. 3.

"The Lesson of the Strikes. III." *Congregationalist,* 27 June 1872, p. 3.
"The Futility of Trades-Unions." *Congregationalist,* 11 July 1872, p. 1.
The Freedom of Faith. Boston: Houghton, Mifflin & Co., 1883.
The Appeal to Life. Boston: Houghton, Mifflin & Co., 1887.
"The Development of Ethical Forces." Conference Sermon. *Proceedings of the Twenty-second National Conference of Charities and Correction, New York, 1895,* pp. 16-27.
Horace Bushnell: Preacher and Theologian. Boston: Houghton, Mifflin & Co., 1899.

PARKHURST, CHARLES H.

"Lay Ministry in New York." *Independent,* 9 January 1890, pp. 1, 2.
"Duty of the Ministry." *Lutheran Observer,* 13 July 1894, p. 1.
"To the Women of America."
    "Andromaniacs." *Ladies Home Journal,* February 1895, p. 15.
    "The Unit of Society." *Ladies' Home Journal,* March 1895, p. 13.
    "The True Mission of Women." *Ladies' Home Journal,* April 1895, p. 15.
    "College Training for Women." *Ladies' Home Journal,* May 1895, p. 15.
    "Women without the Ballot." *Ladies' Home Journal,* June 1895, p. 15.
. . . .
    "The Father's Domestic Headship." *Ladies' Home Journal,* November 1895, p. 15.
"Law and Liberty." *Independent,* 9 May 1895, pp. 1, 2.
Our Fight with Tammany. New York: Charles Scribner's Sons, 1895.
"The Stuff that Makes Young Manhood." *Ladies' Home Journal,* February 1896.
Talks to Young Men. New York: The Century Co., 1897.
Talks to Young Women. New York: The Century Co., 1897.
"The Betterment of Man." Conference Sermon. *Proceedings of the Thirtieth National Conference of Charities and Correction, Atlanta, 1903,* pp. 13-24.
A Little Lower than the Angels. New York: Fleming H. Revell Co., 1908.
My Forty Years in New York. New York: The Macmillan Co., 1923.

* * *

"Dr. Parkhurst's Crusade." *Independent,* 17 March 1892, p. 370.
"Dr. Parkhurst's Victory." *Independent,* 7 April 1892, pp. 478, 479.
Harrower, C.S. "The Police or the People—Which?" *Aggresive Methodism (Christianity City)* 6 (1894): 6, 7.
Drifill, Thomas. "Charles H. Parkhurst." A Poem. *Independent,* 25 April 1895, p. 1.
"Dr. Parkhurst an Example." New York *Christian Advocate,* 4 July 1895, p. 417.

PATTEN, SIMON NELSON

The New Basis of Civilization. The Kennedy Lectures for 1905 in the School of Philanthropy conducted by the New York Charity Organization Society. New York: The Macmillan Co., 1907.
"The Church as a Social Institution." *Independent,* 20 July 1911, pp. 131-133.
The Social Basis of Religion. New York: The Macmillan Co., 1911.

PEABODY, FRANCIS GREENWOOD

"Social Reforms as Subjects of University Study." *Independent,* 14 January 1886, pp. 5, 6.
"The Literature of Social Reform." *Independent,* 8 April 1886, pp. 1, 2.
"The Philosophy of the Social Questions." *Andover Review* 8 (1887): 561-573.
"The Modern Charity Worker." *Charities Review* 2 (1893): 21.
"The Proportion of College-Trained Preachers." *Forum,* September 1894, pp. 30-41.
"Charity and Character." Conference Sermon. *Proceedings of the Twenty-third National Conference of Charities and Correction, Grand Rapids, 1896,* pp. 414-424.
Jesus Christ and the Social Question. New York: The Macmillan Co., 1900.
The Religion of an Educated Man. New York: The Macmillan Co., 1903.
Jesus Christ and the Christian Character: An examination of the Teaching of Jesus in Relation to Some of the Moral Problems of Personal Life. New York: The Macmillan Co., 1905.
Mornings in the College Chapel: Short Addresses to Young Men on Personal Religion. 2nd series. Boston: Houghton, Mifflin & Co., 1907.

The Approach to the Social Question: An Introduction to the Study of Social Ethics. New York: The Macmillan Co., 1909.

Sunday Evenings in College Chapel: Sermons to Young Men. New York: Houghton, Mifflin & Co., 1911.

"Socialization of Religion." *American Journal of Sociology* 18 (1913): 694-705.

Reminiscences of Present-Day Saints. Boston: Houghton, Mifflin & Co., 1927.

* * *

"The Kaiser and Prof. F.G. Peabody," *Congregationalist and Christian World,* 25 November 1905, p. 770.

"Francis Greenwood Peabody." *Harvard Alumni Bulletin,* 8 January 1937, pp. 414, 415.

Herbst, Jurgen. "Frances Greenwood Peabody: Harvard's Theologian of the Social Gospel." *Harvard Theological Review* 54 (1961): 45-69.

RAINSFORD, WILLIAM S.

"Why Not Endow Our Churches?" *Independent,* 22 May 1890, p. 1.

"What Can We Do for the Poor?" *Forum,* April 1891, pp. 115-126.

"Institutionalism Needed, Not Individualism." *Churchman,* 16 January 1892, pp. 62, 63.

"The Endowment of St. George's Church." Letters to the Editor. *Churchman,* 13 February 1892.

The Reasonableness of Faith, and Other Addresses. New York: Doubleday, Page & Co., 1902.

A Preacher's Story of His Work. New York: The Outlook Co., 1904.

The Reasonableness of the Religion of Jesus. Boston: Houghton, Mifflin & Co., 1913.

Story of a Varied Life: An Autobiography. New York: Doubleday, Page & Co., 1922.

* * *

"The Achievement of Dr. Rainsford." *Outlook,* 10 February 1906, p. 291.

RAUSCHENBUSCH, WALTER

"Ideals of Social Reformers." *American Journal of Sociology* 2 (1896): 202-219.

"The Stake of the Church in the Social Movement." *American Journal of Sociology* 3 (1897): 18-30.

Christianity and the Social Crisis. New York: The Macmillan Co., 1907.

Prayers of the Social Awakening. Boston: The Pilgrim Press, 1910.

Christianizing the Social Order. New York: The Macmillan Co., 1912.

"Ye Did It Unto Me." Conference Sermon. *Proceedings of the Thirty-ninth National Conference of Charities and Correction, Cleveland, 1912,* pp. 12-19.

Dare We Be Christians? Boston: The Pilgrim Press, 1914.

A Theology for the Social Gospel. New York: The Macmillan Co., 1917.

STELZLE, CHARLES

"An Institutional Church in a Western Mission." *Open Church* 2 (1898): 358-360.

The Working Man and Social Problems. Chicago: Fleming H. Revell Co., 1903.

Boys of the Street: How to Win Them. New York: Fleming H. Revell Co., 1904.

Messages to Workingmen. New York: Fleming H. Revell Co., 1906.

Christianity's Storm Center: A Study of the Modern City. New York: Fleming H. Revell Co., 1907.

Letters from a Workingman, by an American Mechanic. New York: Fleming H. Revell Co., 1908.

The Church and Labor. Boston: Houghton, Mifflin & Co., 1910.

The Church and the Labor Movement. Published for the Social Service Commission of the Northern Baptist Convention. Philadelphia: American Baptist Publication Society, 1910.

American Social and Religious Conditions. New York: Fleming H. Revell Co., 1912.

The Gospel of Labor. New York: Fleming H. Revell Co., 1912.

* * *

"Mr. Stelzle and the Workingman." *Outlook,* 9 February 1901, pp. 333, 334.

"A Church Envoy to Labor." Boston *Evening Transcript,* 28 January 1905.

STRONG, JOSIAH

Our Country: Its Possible Future and Its Present Crisis. Published for the American Home Missionary Society. New York: Baker & Taylor Co., 1885.

The New Era: Or, The Coming Kingdom. New York: Baker & Taylor Co., 1893.

"The Genius of the Institutional Church." *Christian City* 9 (1897): 25-27.

The Twentieth Century City. New York: Baker & Taylor Co., 1898.

Religious Movements for Social Betterment. New York: Baker & Taylor Co., 1900.
The Times and Young Men. New York: Baker & Taylor Co., 1901.
The Next Great Awakening. New York: Baker & Taylor Co., 1902.
The Challenge of the City. Forward Mission Study Courses, edited under the Direction of the Young People's Missionary Movement. New York: Young People's Missionary Movement, 1907.
My Religion in Everyday Life. New York: Baker & Taylor Co., 1910.

STUCKENBERG, JOHN HENRY WILBURN
Christian Sociology. New York: I.K. Funk & Co., 1880.
"Symposium on the Pulpit: Is the Pulpit Declining in Power? If So, What Is the Remedy?" *Homiletic Review* 10 (1885): 189-195.
"Self-Conscious Protestantism." *Lutheran Observer,* 15 August 1890.
The Church and the Age: Being a Study of the Age and the Adaptation of the Church to Its Needs. Hartford: The Student Publishing Co., 1893.
"The Limit of the Church's Social Activity." *Homiletic Review* 33 (1897): 179-181.
"Social Movements." *Homiletic Review* 33 (1897): 181, 182.
"The Social Problem in the Country." *Homiletic Review* 33 (1897): 467-471.
"Social Study and Social Work." *Homiletic Review* 33 (1897): 79-82, 366-371.
The Social Problem. York, Pa.: Social Problem Publishing Co., 1897.
Introduction to the Study of Sociology. New York: A. C. Armstrong & Son, 1898.
"Religious and Social Thought and Movement at the Close of the Nineteenth Century." *Homiletic Review* 40 (1900): 552-557.
Sociology, the Science of Human Society. New York: G.P. Putnam's Sons, 1903.

* * *

Evjen, John O. *The Life of J.H.W. Stuckenberg: Theologian—Philosopher—Sociologist.* Minneapolis: The Lutheran Free Church Publishing Co., 1938.

TAYLOR, GRAHAM
"The Hartford Pastors' Mission." *Congregationalist,* 28 April 1887.
Five Years' Growth: A Sketch of the Evangelistic Work Centering at the Fourth Church, Hartford, Conn. Hartford, 1889. Chicago. Newberry Library. Graham Taylor Collection.
"Dr. Taylor's Farewell." Hartford *Courant,* 19 September 1892.
"Social Function of the Church." *American Journal of Sociology* 5 (1899): 305-317.
Religion in Social Action. New York: Dodd, Mead & Co., 1913.
Pioneering on Social Frontiers. Chicago: University of Chicago Press, 1930.

* * *

Bridgman, Howard A. "Graham Taylor: Apostle of Social Christianity." *Congregationalist and Christian World,* 1 April 1905, pp. 426-428.

TOLMAN, WILLIAM HOWE
"The Educational Value of Reform Movements." *Congregationalist,* 24 August 1893, p. 246.
"The Fight for Municipal Reform in New York City." *Congregationalist,* 30 November 1893, p. 784.
Municipal Reform Movements in the United States: The Textbook of the New Reformation. New York: Fleming H. Revell Co., 1895.
Industrial Betterment. New York: The Social Service Press, 1900.
The Better New York. Coauthored by Charles Hemstreet, with an afterword by Josiah Strong. New York: Baker & Taylor Co., 1904.

TUCKER, WILLIAM JEWETT
"Some Present Questions in Evangelism." *Andover Review* 1 (1884): 233-244.
"Social Problems in the Pulpit: Dr. Newman Smyth's Sermons to Workingmen." *Andover Review* 3 (1885): 297-302.
"Christianity and Its Modern Competitors." *Andover Review* 6 (1886): 510-514.
"Christianity and Its Modern Competitors. II. Social Ethics." *Andover Review* 7 (1887): 64-80.
"The Gospel of Wealth." *Andover Review* 15 (1891): 631-645.
"The Authority of the Pulpit in a Time of Critical Research and Social Confusion." *Andover Review* 16 (1891): 384-402.

"Social Christianity: The Andover House Association." *Andover Review* 17 (1892): 82-86.
"The Spiritual Life of the Modern City." *Congregationalist,* 31 December 1896, pp. 1038-1040.
Personal Power: Counsels to Young Men. Boston: Houghton, Mifflin & Co., 1910.
Public Mindedness: An Aspect of Citizenship Considered in Various Addresses Given While President of Dartmouth College. Concord: The Rumford Press, 1910.
My Generation: An Autobiographical Interpretation. New York: Houghton, Mifflin & Co., 1919.

VINCENT, JOHN HEYL

"An Alliance for Popular Education." *Independent,* 10 July 1884, pp. 7-9.
The Chautauqua Movement. With an introduction by Lewis Miller. Boston: Chautauqua Press, 1886.
"The Chautauqua Idea." *Christian Union,* 31 January 1889, p. 154.
"The Minister and Social Problems. I." *Independent,* 17 March 1892, pp. 361, 362.
"The Minister and Social Problems. II." *Independent,* 24 March 1892, pp. 399, 400.
"The Coming Church." *Independent,* 7 July 1892.

* * *

Vincent, Leon H. *John Heyl Vincent: A Biographical Sketch.* New York: The Macmillan Co., 1925.
Wilkinson, William Cleaver. "John H. Vincent." *Independent,* 10 January 1884, pp. 3, 4.

WOODS, ROBERT A.

English Social Movements. New York: Charles Scribner's Sons, 1891.
"Working Men: One Thing to Say to Them." *Congregationalist,* 9 March 1893, pp. 376, 377.
The Poor in Great Cities. New York: Charles Scribner's Sons, 1895.
The City Wilderness: A Settlement Study by Residents and Associates of the South End House. Boston: Houghton, Mifflin & Co., 1898.

Charities, Welfare and Educational Work

"A Wind of God for City Children." [Outdoor beds for tenement children]. *Independent,* 9 October 1913, p. 90.
"Charities." [Industrial Christian Alliance]. *Independent,* 15 March 1894, p. 14.
"Christian Workers at New Haven." *Congregationalist,* 21 November 1895, pp. 779, 780.
"Church Club." *Churchman,* 6 February 1892, pp. 158, 159; 9 April 1892, pp. 448-450.
"Church Club of New York." Annual Dinner. *Churchman,* 9 February 1895, p. 199.
"City Missions in New York." *Outlook,* 22 April 1893, p. 775.
"East Side Work in This City [New York]." *Churchman,* 24 December 1892, p. 849.
"Fresh Air and Fresh Money." *Christian City* 11 (1899): 110, 111.
"Guild of St. Barnabus." [Fellowship of nurses]. *Churchman,* 2 January 1892, pp. 11, 12.
Hart, Hastings H. "The Children's Aid Society in the West." *Independent,* 15 May 1884, p. 3.
"Letter from New York." A self-supporting "penny restaurant" for the decent poor. *Congregationalist,* 30 January 1878, p. 1.
"Letter from New York." Mr. Comstock's "Society for the Suppression of Vice." *Congregationalist,* 13 February 1878, p. 1.
"Letter from New York." [The Good Samaritan Christian Restaurant]. *Congregationalist,* 11 January 1882, p. 1.
Means, D. McG. "Private Aid to Public Charities." *Andover Review* 4 (1885): 220-230.
"Methods of Charity." *Independent,* 11 January 1894, p. 15.
"More About Our Fresh Air Work." *Christian City* 11 (1899): 142.
"New York's Charities." *Lutheran Observer,* 19 April 1889, p. 1.
"Outlook in Education." [Drexel Institute of Art, Science, and Industry, in Philadelphia]. *Outlook,* 2 January 1892, p. 35.
"Pratt Institute, Brooklyn, N.Y.: Its Aim and Scope." *Lutheran Observer,* 20 July 1894, p. 6.
"Religious Notes." [Benefit fund in a church in Tabor, Iowa]. *Independent,* 15 March 1894, p. 13.
Riis, Jacob A. "The Heart of New York." *Independent,* 4 December 1913, pp. 449, 450.
Schodde, George H. "Religious Work among the Immigrants." *Independent,* 7 March 1895, p. 313.
Shaw, Albert, "The Higher Life of New York City." *Outlook,* 25 January 1896, pp. 132-139.
"Social Statistics of a City Parish." *Independent,* 10 January 1895, p. 49.

Stone, Melville E. "The Higher Life of Chicago." *Outlook,* 22 February 1896, pp. 326-331.
"The Tenement House." *Presbyterian,* 28 February 1894, p. 9.
Tobey, R.B. "Concerning Charity: Fad, Fact, Fallacy." *Congregationalist,* 21 December 1893, pp. 923, 924.
West, Frances. "Woman's Place and Work: In the Midst of Them." *Churchman,* 16 July 1898, p. 96.
Wingate, Charles F. "How to Make New York a Better City." *Aggressive Methodism (Christian City)* 6 (1894): 4-6.
"Work of the Church Club of Philadelphia." *Churchman,* 17 December 1898, p. 889.

Charity Organization

"A New Method of Charity Work: The Buffalo Plan." *Outlook,* 11 July 1896, p. 65.
Bishop, Samuel H. "The Church and Charity." *American Journal of Sociology* 18 (1912): 369-380.
———. "The New Movement in Charity." *American Journal of Sociology* 7 (1902): 595-610.
Bulkey, Edwin A. "Organized Charity in the Church." *Independent,* 20 November 1884, pp. 5, 6.
Caldwell, J.C. "Pauperism and Charity." *Lutheran Quarterly* 24 (1894): 39-48.
"Churches and Soup-Houses." *Independent,* 19 July 1894.
Denny, Collins. "Bear Ye One Another's Burdens." Conference Sermon. *Proceedings of the Twenty-first National Conference of Charities and Correction, Nashville, 1894,* pp. 214-225.
Hopkins, Henry. "The Church and Charity." *Independent,* 11 February 1892, p. 2.
Hoskins, F.D. "Pauperism and Its Treatment." *American Church Review* 31 (1879): 130-145.
Jenkins, J.L. "Professionalism in Christian Service." *Congregationalist,* 3 April 1890, p. 2.
"Notes by the Way." [The Buffalo plan of cooperation between churches and charities]. *Churchman,* 17 December 1898, pp. 883, 884.
Paine, Robert Treat. "The Relationship between the Church and the Associated Charities." *Open Church* 1 (1897): 196-198.
Pond, C.N. "Charity Organization Principles Applied to Mission Work." In *Proceedings of the Twenty-seventh National Conference of Charities and Correction, Topeka, 1900,* pp. 271-277.
Potter, Henry C. *Addresses to Women Engaged in Church Work.* Published for the Church Work Association. New York: E.P. Dutton & Co., 1887.
"Practical Co-operation in Charity." *Churchman,* 24 December 1898, p. 930.
Spalding, John Lancaster. "Charity and Justice." Conference Sermon. *Proceedings of the Twenty-ninth National Conference of Charities and Correction, Detroit, 1902,* pp. 13-26.
Stimson, Henry A. "The New Charity." *Andover Review* 3 (1885): 107-120.
Warner, Amos G. "Our Charities and Our Churches." In *Proceedings of the Sixteenth National Conference of Charities and Correction, San Francisco, 1889,* pp. 36-41.

Church and Labor

Adams, George M. "Capital and Labor: What Has the Church to Do?" *Congregationalist,* 12 June 1878, p. 2.
Adams, Henry Carter. "Discontent among the Laboring Classes." *Congregationalist,* 25 January 1882, p. 2.
Albert, Charles S. "The Church and the Labor Problem." *Lutheran Quarterly* 17 (1887): 248-259.
Bradford, A.H. "Why the Artisan Classes Neglect the Church: In Two Papers." I. "The Facts." *Christian Union,* 2 July 1885, p. 7. II. "Remedies." *Christian Union,* 9 July 1885, pp. 7, 8.
Brewster, Chauncey B. "Industrial War or Peace." *Independent,* 13 July 1911, pp. 75-78.
"Chicago Church Club: The Church and the Workingman." *Churchman,* 24 April 1892, pp. 517, 518.
"Chicago Church Club: Adjourned Meeting." *Churchman,* 7 May 1892, pp. 584, 585.
Cole, William I. "Duty of the Church to the Workingman." *Open Church* 1 (1897): 100, 101.
Cordley, Richard. "Capital or Labor." *Congregationalist,* 2 August 1882, p. 1.
Crafts, Wilbur F. "Reasons for the Rest Day: The Workingman's College." *Lutheran Observer,* 6 June 1890, p. 3.
Eliot, Charles W. "Capital and Labor Far Apart." Boston *Evening Transcript,* 16 January 1904.
Gutman, Herbert G. "Protestantism and the American Labor Movement: The Christian Spirit in the Gilded Age." In *The National Temper: Readings in American History,* edited by Lawrence W. Levine and Robert Middlekauff, pp. 235-262. New York: Harcourt, Brace & World, 1968.
Hoadley, James H. "Workingmen in City Churches." *Independent,* 12 January 1888, p. 5.

Hollister, Alonzo Giles. "The Remedy for the Strife." *Independent,* 7 February 1895, p. 166.
Huntington, Frederic Dan. "Some Points in the Labor Question." *Church Review* 58 (1886): 1-20.
———. "Relations of Employer and Employed." *Churchman,* 20 August 1892, pp. 217, 218.
———. "The Causes and Losses of Strikes." *Independent,* 7 February 1895, p. 166.
Huntington, James O.S. "Congress of the Knights of Labor." *Churchman,* 13 February 1892, p. 190.
Irvine, A. Fitzgerald. "A University Labor Union." *Outlook,* 20 January 1906, pp. 131, 132.
Johnson, Herbert S. "The Key to Universal Social Equilibrium." *Independent,* 2 May 1895, pp. 581, 582.
"Labor Day and the Church." *Congregationalist and Christian World,* 2 September 1905, p. 307.
"Labor Movement in the Church." *Presbyterian,* 14 May 1887, pp. 10, 11.
"Labor or Capital." *Presbyterian,* 3 October 1894, pp. 4-6.
Osborne, C.P. "The Labor Question." *Congregationalist,* 2 October 1878, p. 1.
"Religion as a Factor in Business." *Congregationalist,* 9 October 1890, p. 4.
Richards, M.H. "A Penny a Day." *Lutheran Quarterly* 17 (1887): 102-118.
———. "Labor: A Revolution and a Problem." *Lutheran Quarterly* 23 (1893): 55-68.
Shortt, Adam. "The Evolution of the Relation between Capital and Labor." *Andover Review* 11 (1889): 144-161.
Smyth, Newman. "The Relation of Christianity to Labor." *Christian Union,* 23 July 1885, p. 25.
Stimson, Henry A. "The Confessions of Business Men." *Congregationalist,* 11 March 1886, p. 2.
Stryker, M.W. "Rights and Duties of Craft and Capital." *Independent,* 2 May 1895, pp. 579, 580.
"Srikes and Their Remedies." *Christian Union,* 21 February 1889, p. 227.
Sturtevant, J.M. "What Is the Remedy?" *Congregationalist,* 3 April 1878, p. 2.
Swift, Morrison I. "Unfair Burdens on Real Production." *Andover Review* 13 (1890): 139-150.
———. "The Working Population of Cities and What the Universities Owe Them." *Andover Review* 13 (1890): 589-613.
———. "The Halo of Industrial Idleness." *Andover Review* 16 (1891): 558-568.
"The Church and Labor." *Congregationalist and Christian World,* 30 December 1905.
"The Church and the Laboring Classes." 2nd annual report of the Massachusetts Bureau of Labor Statistics. *American Church Review* 24 (1872): 1-14.
"'The Churches' and Industrial Discontent." *Churchman,* 20 August 1892, pp. 212, 213.
"The Labor Problem." *Presbyterian,* 23 April 1887, p. 10.
Warner, Elmer E. "The Labor Problem: A Voice from the Bench." *Christian Union,* 24 December 1885, p. 8.
Washburn, George. "Christianity and the Labor Question." *Independent,* 22 October 1884, pp. 2, 3.
Willett, J. "Letter from a Workingman." *Christian Union,* 29 October 1885, pp. 7, 8.
"Workmen Criticize the Church." Boston *Evening Transcript,* 12 January 1901.

Church Federation

"A Federate Summer School of Theology." *Congregationalist and Christian World,* 19 August 1905, p. 251.
"An American Forward Movement." *Outlook,* 5 January 1901, p. 9.
Anthony, Alfred Williams. "A Practical Church Federation." *Independent,* 23 March 1905, pp. 665-667.
Berle, A.A. "Inter-Seminary Missionary Alliance." *Independent,* 11 November 1885, p. 14.
Brodie, Andrew W. "Successful Ways of Solving the Country Church Problem." *Congregationalist and Christian World,* 22 July 1905, p. 115.
Brown, William Montgomery. *The Church for Americans.* New York: Thomas Whittaker, 1895.
———. *The Level Plan for Church Union.* New York: Thomas Whittaker, 1910.
"Closer Federation of City Work." *Congregationalist and Christian World,* 3 June 1905, p. 744.
Crafts, Wilbur F. "The Moody Conference of Christian Workers." *Lutheran Observer,* 22 August 1890, p. 1.
Faville, John. "Our Overchurched Communities." *Independent,* 6 August 1884, pp. 5, 6.
"For Federation in Christian Work." *Christian City* 12 (1900): 19, 20.
Hull, William E. "The American Inter-Seminary Missionary Alliance." *Lutheran Quarterly* 16 (1886): 549-553.
Huntington, William Reed. *The Church-Idea: An Essay towards Unity.* New York: E.P. Dutton & Co., 1870.
"Inter-Church Conference on Federation." *Congregationalist and Christian World,* 25 November 1905, pp. 752-754.

Jackson, J.C. "Benefits of a City Evangelization Union." New York *Christian Advocate,* 17 October 1895, p. 668.

Kennedy, Albert J. "Religious Overlapping." *Independent,* 9 April 1908, pp. 795-799.

Laidlaw, Walter. "A Plea and Plan for a Co-operative Church Parish in Cities." *American Journal of Sociology* 3 (1898): 795-808.

———. "Christ and the City." *Christian City* 10 (1898): 500-503.

———. "The Federation of the Churches: What It Is and What It Does in New York City." *Christian City* 10 (1898): 388-393.

"Leading Participants in the Inter-Church Federation Conference." *Congregationalist and Christian World,* 4 November 1905, pp. 634, 635.

Macy, Herbert. "Co-operation and Federation." *Congregationalist,* 19 June 1890.

Miller, A.B. "Mr. Moody's Convention of Christian Workers." *Lutheran Observer,* 30 August 1889, p. 2.

"Net Results of the Inter-Church Federation Conference." *Congregationalist and Christian World,* 2 December 1905, pp. 800, 801.

Newton, William Wilberforce. "The Congress of Churches at Cleveland." *Independent,* 3 June 1886, p. 17.

Parker, E.P. "The American Congress of Religions." *Independent,* 2 May 1884, p. 14.

Pentecost, George F. "The American Congress of Churches." *Independent,* 8 May 1884, pp. 2, 3.

"Reciprocity between Denominations." *Congregationalist and Christian World,* 15 July 1905, p. 94.

Root, E. Tallmadge. "The Co-operative Parish Plan in a Typical City: The Actual Workings of Federation in Providence, R.I." *Congregationalist and Christian World,* 4 November 1905, pp. 636, 637.

Seward, Theodore F. "The Brotherhood of Christian Unity: Progress of the Movement." *Outlook,* 30 January 1892, p. 213.

"Social Unions and Christian Fellowship." *Independent,* 3 April 1890, p. 16.

Stryker, M. Woolsey. "Shall We Burn Five Thousand Churches?" *Congregationalist and Christian World,* 4 November 1905, p. 628.

Taylor, William R. "Union Evangelistic Movement in Philadelphia." *Independent,* 25 November 1886, pp. 16, 17.

"The Church I Am Looking For, By One Who Is Seeking a Church Home." *Independent,* 13 February 1908, pp. 344-346.

"The Federation of Churches." *Outlook,* 16 February 1901, pp. 379, 380.

"The General Convention and Christian Unity." *Churchman,* 8 October 1898, p. 473.

"The Religious Movement." *Presbyterian,* 8 January 1887, pp. 10, 11.

"The Union Movement in New York." *Lutheran Observer,* 4 April 1890, p. 2.

"Union Efforts of Churches." *Congregationalist,* 26 January 1893, p. 126.

Williams, Leighton. "Federation of Churches and Christian Workers in New York City." *Open Church* 1 (1897): 95, 96.

Wolf, E.J. "Denominational Co-operation: A Plea for the Immigrants." *Independent,* 5 April 1888, pp. 4, 5.

Institutional Churches

Abbott, Mrs. Lyman. "The Social Life of a Church." *Ladies' Home Journal,* November 1895, p. 18.

"A California Institutional Church." *Open Church* 2 (1898): 363, 364.

"A Cincinnati Institutional Church." *Open Church* 2 (1898): 279-281.

"Actors' Church Alliance." *Outlook,* 9 March 1901, p. 566.

"Advertizing the Gospel." *Independent,* 26 January 1905, pp. 196-201.

All Souls Church. *Annuals.* 24 vols. Chicago, 1884-1907.

———. *The Abraham Lincoln Centre and All Souls Church Annual.* Containing a Summary of the Work for 25 Years, 1882-1907. Chicago, 1908.

———. *The Abraham Lincoln Centre and All Souls Church Annual.* Reports of 1909. Chicago, 1910.

"An Aggressive Church [The Tabernacle Church in Jersey City]." *Congregationalist,* 5 June 1890, p. 2.

"An East Side Problem and an Attempt at Its Solution." *Christian City* 12 (1900): 144-150.

"An Encouraging Comparison;" *Christian City* 11 (1899): 13.

"An Hour at the 'Mothers' Seaside Home' at Long Branch." *Christian City* 11 (1899): 114.

"Annual Convention of the Open and Institutional Church League." *Christian City* 9 (1897): 31-36.

"Annual Meeting of the Girls' Friendly Society in America." *Churchman,* 19 November 1898, p. 735.

"Armour Manual Training School." *Congregationalist,* 12 January 1893, p. 56.

"A Southern Institutional Church." *Congregationalist,* 14 December 1893, pp. 896, 897.

"A Victorious Year at Cornell Memorial Church." *Christian City* 12 (1900): 90, 91.

"A Working Church [Church of the Holy Communion]." *Christian Union*, 29 January 1885, p. 25.

"A Working Church [Calvary Protestant Episcopal Church in New York City]." *Christian Union*, 26 December 1891, p. 1286.

"A Wonderful Parish [St. George's, New York]." *Churchman*, 30 January 1892, p. 132.

Ayers, M.C. "The Work of Berkeley Temple." *Christian Union*, 6 December 1888, p. 653.

Baldwin, William. "The Gospel of Ministration in a Methodist Episcopal Church [Frank Mason North's Calvary Church]." *Christian City* 12 (1900): 4, 5.

Ballantine, John Winthrop. "A Great Church Enterprise." *Independent*, 21 February 1884, pp. 4, 5.

"Baptist Temple, Philadelphia." *Outlook*, 22 February 1896, p. 349.

Belcher, F.J. "The Metropolitan Temple Parish, New York." *Open Church* 2 (1898): 343-347.

Besant, Walter and Rice, James. *All Sorts and Conditions of Men: An Impossible Story.* The "Palace of Delight" in London. New York: Harper & Bros., 1882.

Betts, Lillian W. "Sunday in the Tenement. I. As It Is." *Outlook*, 16 January 1892, pp. 108, 109.

———. "Sunday in the Tenement-House. II. As It Might Be." *Outlook*, 23 January 1892, pp. 156-158.

"Below Fourteenth Street." *Christian City* 11 (1899): 1.

Bottome, Margaret. "The King's Daughters." *Ladies' Home Journal*, January to November 1895.

Bridgman, Howard Allen. "Have We Too Many Churches?" *Andover Review* 17 (1892): 488-495.

"Broadway Tabernacle." *Outlook*, 2 February 1901, p. 240.

"Brotherhood of St. Andrew in Annual Convention." *Churchman*, 8 October 1898, pp. 481-485.

Buckham, M.H. "Lay Theology." *Andover Review* 1 (1884): 149-159.

Burk, Addison R. "The Drexel Institute." *Outlook*, 6 February 1892, pp. 252-254.

Burr, Everett D. "Methods of an Open and Institutional Church." *Open Church* 1 (1897): 97-99.

Byles, A. Holden. "The 'Pleasant Sunday Afternoon' Movement." *Open Church* 1 (1897): 146-149.

———. "The P.S.A. Movement in England." *Independent*, 21 February 1895, pp. 241, 242.

Cadman, S. Parkes. "The Advance Movement of the Church in Great Cities." *Christian City* 9 (1897): 278-282.

Chapman, J. Wilbur. "Bethany Church of Philadelphia." *Chautauquan* 12 (1891): 470-473.

Clark, Francis E. "A Quarter-Century of Christian Endeavor." *Outlook*, 13 January 1906, pp. 80-84.

———. "The Christian Endeavor Movement." *Lutheran Observer*, 26 July 1889, p. 4.

———. "The Origin and Growth of the Christian Endeavor Movement." *Independent*, 7 July 1892, p. 930.

Clemens, Samuel Langhorne [Mark Twain]. "A New Beecher Church." In *A Curious Dream: and Other Sketches*, pp. 24-38. London: G. Routledge & Sons, 1872.

Coleman, Mary Winniett. "Woman's Place and Work: Parish Work. VI. Grace Church, Chicago." *Churchman*, 9 April 1892, p. 467.

Collins, John C. "Ministry to the Poor." *New Englander* 38 (1879): 169-183.

Converse, John H. "From a Layman's Standpoint: The Churches and Their Work." *Christian City* 9 (1897): 40, 41.

Cooke, George Willis. "The Institutional Church." *New England Magazine* 14 (1896): 645-660.

Cooper, James W. "Child Nurture in the Church." *Andover Review* 2 (1884): 47-57.

Cox, Herbert Sydney. "The New Broadway Tabernacle." *Congregationalist and Christian World*, 4 March 1905, pp. 293, 294.

———. "A Genuine People's Palace." *Congregationalist and Christian World*, 8 July 1905, pp. 48, 49.

Craven, Ellyn. "Woman's Place and Work: Parish Work. V. St. Bartholomew's Church." *Churchman*, 20 February 1892, pp. 238, 239.

Cuyler, Theodore L. "Forerunners of the Christian Endeavor Society." *Independent*, 7 July 1892, pp. 930-935.

"David H. Greer." *Outlook*, 4 January 1896, p. 11.

Dent, Elmer A. "The People's Forward Movement at 61st Street Methodist Episcopal Church." *Christian City* 12 (1900): 36-39.

Devins, John Bancroft. "For an Open Church: Earnest Work at the Convention of the Institutional League." *Christian City* 11 (1899): 194-197.

Dewey, Harry P. "The Plant of a Working Church [Plymouth Congregational Church, Minneapolis]." *Independent*, 10 November 1910, pp. 1026-1030.

Dickinson, Charles A. "The Church and Secular Life." *Christian City* 9 (1897): 3.

———. "The Problem of the Modern City Church." *Andover Review* 12 (1889): 355-372.

Dike, Samuel W.; Sheldon, Charles M.; Allen, M.J.; and Merriam, Charles Loveland. "The Problem of the Country Church." *Andover Review* 10 (1888): 379-395.

"Dr. Deems and the American Institute of Philosophy." New York *Christian Advocate,* 25 July 1895, p. 465.

Dunning, A.E. "The Expansion of the Local Church." *Andover Review* 17 (1892): 12-23.

"Editorial." [The Scudders of Jersey City]. *Christian Union,* 21 November 1891, p. 967.

"Editorial Notes." [Methodism in the great cities]. *Independent,* 22 February 1894, p. 12.

"Editorial Notes." [Rev. Tyndall and the People's Tabernacle]. *Open Church* 2 (1898): 370.

[Editorial on the Institutional Church]. *Churchman,* 15 October 1898, pp. 514, 515.

"Editorial: The Enlargement of the Function of the Local Church." *Andover Review* 5 (1886): 67-65.

Ellis, William T. "Christian Endeavor and Higher Education." *Independent,* 18 April 1895, p. 521.

––––––. "The New Era of Church Work in Boston." *Open Church* 1 (1897): 174-185.

"Exodus from the Tenements." *Churchman,* 23 July 1892, p. 92.

"Fifty Years of Beginnings." *Outlook,* 19 December 1896, p. 1144.

Foster, William W. "The Kindergarten of the Church." *Open Church* 1 (1897): 84-89.

"Four Institutional Churches."

    I. Bourne, Henry E. "St. George's, New York." *Congregationalist,* 13 April 1893, pp. 578, 579.

    II. "The Fourth Church, Hartford." *Congregationalist,* 20 April 1893, pp. 619, 620.

    III. "The Jersey City Tabernacle." *Congregationalist,* 27 April 1893, pp. 659, 660.

    IV. "Berkeley Temple, Boston." *Congregationalist,* 4 May 1893, pp. 699, 700.

Fourth Congregational Church, Hartford. *Seventy-Five Years and the Present Outlook, 1832-1907.* Published in connection with the observance of the 75th anniversary of the founding of the church. Chicago. Newberry Library. Graham Taylor Collection.

Fourth Congregational Church, Hartford. *Yearbook for 1890 and Report of Evangelistic Work for Year Ending 28 February 1891 with Appendix.* Hartford: Case, Lockwood & Brainard Co., 1891.

"Fourth Convention of the Institutional Church League." *Outlook,* 31 October 1896, p. 793.

Folsom, C.M. "The Institutional Work of Hampton." *Open Church* 2 (1898): 319-323.

Foust, John J. "A Strategic Center for a Larger Work." *Christian City* 10 (1898): 453-457.

Gardiner, Edwin J. "Church Work among Young Men." *Church Review* 49 (1887): 484-500.

Gilbert, Levi. "The Down-Town Church Again." *Christian City* 10 (1898): 380-383.

"Glimpses of Work at Allen Street Memorial." *Christian City* 11 (1899): 105, 106.

Gray, Arthur E. "Pilgrim Institutional Church, Worcester, Mass." *Open Church* 2 (1898): 368, 369.

Greer, David H. "Medical Charities in Relation to Religious Societies." In *Proceedings of the Twenty-fifth National Conference of Charities and Correction, New York, 1898,* pp. 332-336.

Hall, Newton M. "Church Industrial Schools." *Christian Union,* 7 March 1889, p. 295.

Hamlen, Ewing W. "How We Founded the Boys' Brigade." *Independent,* 18 April 1895, pp. 513-514.

Haynes, Emory J. "Tremont Temple: A Church in Boston." *Chautauquan* 12 (1890): 48-51.

Helms, E.J. "Morgan Chapel, Boston." *Christian City* 11 (1899): 60-65.

Howard, R.H. "The Genius of Methodism." New York *Christian Advocate,* 30 May 1895, p. 343.

"How to Empty a Church Evenings." *Christian Union,* 21 November 1891, p. 991.

Huntington, James O.S. "The Brotherhood of St. Andrew." *Churchman,* 10 December 1892, pp. 797-799.

Hyde, C.M. "New Times, New Men, New Methods." *Congregationalist,* 23 October 1890, p. 2.

"Industrial Christian Alliance." *Lutheran Observer,* 19 January 1894, p. 10.

"Institutional Churches." *Presbyterian,* 17 January 1894, pp. 8, 9.

"Judson Memorial." *Christian Union,* 21 March 1889, p. 372.

Kakel, F.W. "The Boys' Brigade: The Results in a Lutheran Church." *Lutheran Observer,* 11 March 1898, p. 7.

"Keeping the Church Doors Open." *Congregationalist,* 20 February 1890, p. 4.

Kelsey, Henry H. "The Christian Industrial League." *Open Church* 1 (1897): 137, 138.

Kent, William. "Jenkin Lloyd Jones." *American Magazine,* July 1910, pp. 320-322.

"Kitchen-Garden Schools." *Christian Union,* 2 July 1885, p. 25.

"Lay Criticism on the Ministry and the Methods of Church Work." *Homiletic Review* 8 (1884): 291-293; 293-295; 351-355; 411, 412; 412-414; 527, 528, 588-591; 648-650; 650-655; 769-772; 829, 830; 10 (1885): 444, 445; 11 (1886): 264, 265; 12 (1886): 215, 216.

Lawrence, E.A. "An Endeavor Experiment with Social Christianity." *Congregationalist,* 27 July 1893, pp. 117, 118.

"Letter from New York." Dr. Deem's Church of the Strangers. *Congregationalist,* 9 October 1878, p. 1.

"Letter from New York." The Tabernacle Church in Jersey City. *Congregationalist,* 20 March 1878, p. 1.

Littlefield, Charles A. "A Problem that Must and Can Be Solved." *Christian City* 12 (1900): 59-64.

Loucks, W.E. "Institutional Work in Beacon Church." *Presbyterian,* 25 July 1894, p. 16.

MacAdam, George. *The Little Church Around the Corner.* New York: G.P. Putnam's Sons, 1925.

"Medical Charity." *Outlook,* 16 March 1901, p. 615.

McCulloch, James E. *The Open Church for the Unchurched: or, How to Reach the Masses.* New York: Fleming H. Revell Co., 1905.

"Milford Holiday House." *Churchman,* 17 September 1898, pp. 290, 291.

Miller, A.H. "The Niedringhaus Memorial Church in St. Louis." *Aggressive Methodism (Christian City)* 6 (1894): 4.

Miller, J.R. "The Spirit of the Institutional Church." *Open Church* 1 (1897): 75-89.

Mills, Charles S. "The Institutional Church." *Bibliotheca Sacra* 49 (1892): 453-470.

"Ministry of a Brooklyn Church." *Christian City* 10 (1898): 342-345.

Murphy, Edgar Gardner. "Reconstruction in Religion." *Outlook,* 23 March 1901, p. 682.

Murray, W.H.H. "A Metropolitan Church." *Congregationalist,* 11 December 1873, p. 1.

"New Era of Church Work: Ruggles Street Baptist Church, Boston." *Open Church* 2 (1898): 205-213.

"Newsboys' and Bootblacks' Thanksgiving." *Congregationalist,* 6 December 1882, p.2.

"New System in City Churches." *Scribner's Monthly,* June 1874, pp. 241, 242.

North, Frank Mason. "The New Era of Church Work in New York." *Christian City* 9 (1894): 1-24.

Oliver, Charles A. "Christian Endeavor and the Evangelization of the Masses." *Presbyterian,* 7 November 1894, p. 19.

Oliver, William James. "St. Bartholomew's Parish House Work." *Aggressive Methodism (Christian City)* 6 (1894): 5, 6.

"One Down-Town Street." *Christian City* 11 (1899): 19.

"175 Years at Hopewell Church." *Christian Intelligencer,* 4 January 1933, p. 7.

"Open or Institutional Church League." *Aggressive Methodism (Christian City)* 6 (1894): 6, 7.

"Open and Institutional Church League." *Congregationalist,* 21 November 1895, p. 778.

Palmer, Frederic. "The Contribution of the Episcopal Church to Modern Religious Life." *Andover Review* 17 (1892): 376-392.

Partridge, Warren G. "An Institutional Church." *Christian City* 11 (1899): 118-121.

"Philadelphia: Its Aggressive Work."*Aggressive Methodism (Christian City)* 6 (1894): 3.

"Platform of the Open and Institutional Church League." *Open Church* 1 (1897): 4.

"Pleasant Friday Nights." *Christian City* 11 (1899): 43.

"Progressive Methods of Church Work."

    I. Alden, Edmund K. "The Jersey City Tabernacle and People's Palace." *Christian Union,* 21 November 1891, pp. 992, 993.

    II. Manson, George J. "Two Model Parish Houses." *Christian Union,* 28 November 1891, p. 1046.

    III. "A New Departure." *Christian Union,* 5 December 1891, p. 1100.

    IV. Bradford, Amory H. "A Surburban Field." *Christian Union,* 12 December 1891, p. 1178.

    V. "Week-Day Work in a City Church." *Outlook,* 2 January 1892, pp. 30, 31.

    VI. Alden, Edmund K. "The Berkeley Temple of Today." *Outlook,* 6 December 1888, p. 78.

    VII. Powell, S.W. "A Group of Schools." *Outlook,* 6 February 1892, pp. 271, 272.

    VIII. Campbell, James M. "Two Representative Missions of Chicago." *Outlook,* 27 February 1892, pp. 414, 415.

    . . . .

    XV. Alden, Edmund K. "The Temple, Philadelphia." *Outlook,* 18 March 1893, pp. 508, 509.

    XVI. Manson, George J. "How Rich and Poor Meet Together at Asbury Church." *Outlook,* 8 April 1893, pp. 665, 666.

Quint, A.R. "Concerning Club-Houses." *Congregationalist,* 27 March 1898, p. 1.

"Readjustment of City Churches." *Andover Review* 9 (1888): 76-79.

"Religious Notes." [Charles L. Thompson and Madison Ave. Presbyterian Church]. *Independent,* 18 January 1894, p. 13.

"Report of the Annual Convention of the Open and Institutional Church League, November 2 and 3, 1898." *Open Church* 3 (1899): 22, 23.

Ross, Edward A. "The Educational Function of the Church." *Outlook,* 28 August 1897, pp. 1036-1040.

Rowe, O.M.E. "Ethics of the Cooking Schools." *Congregationalist,* 26 April 1882, p. 1.

———. "Penny Savings." *Congregationalist,* 11 September 1890, p. 2.

Scudder, John L. "The People's Palace of Jersey City." *Charities Review* 1 (1891): 90-92.

Shaw, John Balcom. "Men and the Church." *Independent,* 28 February 1895, pp. 262, 263.

Smith, Charles Sprague. "A Creedless Church for a Creedless People." *Independent,* 2 January 1908, pp. 31-33.

"Some Great Working Churches."

    Dyer, E. Porter. "Hope Church, Springfield." *Congregationalist,* 4 February 1886, p. 1.

    Kellogg, Mrs. S.B. "Pilgrim Church, St. Louis." *Congregationalist,* 11 February 1886, p.2.

    Gilbert, Simon. "Plymouth Church, Minneapolis." *Congregationalist,* 18 February 1886, p. 1.

    Bisbee, M.D. "The First Church, Lowell." *Congregationalist,* 25 February 1886, p. 1.

    Maynard, Lasalle A. "The Central Congregational Church of Brooklyn." *Congregationalist,* 4 March 1886, p. 1.

    Gilbert, Simeon. "The First Church, Chicago." *Congregationalist,* 11 March 1886, p. 1.

    Holbrook, J.C. "The First Church, Oakland." *Congregationalist,* 18 March 1886, p. 2.

Spencer, Joseph Jansen. "Open and Institutional Work in the Village Church: A New England Experiment." *Open Church* 3 (1899): 3-10.

Stahley, G.D. "Empty Pews: How Shall We Fill Them?" *Lutheran Quarterly* 18 (1888): 341-351.

Stall, Sylvanus. "Methods of Church Work." *Christian City* 9 (1897): 28-30.

Stimson, Henry A. "Effective Evening Services." *Independent,* 31 March 1910, pp. 689-691.

"Symposium on the Institutional Church."

    I. Thompson, Charles L. "An Agency in Accord with the Spirit and Method of the Gospel." *Homiletic Review* 32 (1896): 560-564.

    II. Mallard, R.Q. "Not the Ideal Church." *Homiletic Review* 33 (1897): 84-89.

    III. Conwell, Russell H: "As a Factor in City Evangelization." *Homiletic Review* 33 (1897): 184, 185.

    IV. Mills, Charles S. "As a Factor in City Evangelization." *Homiletic Review* 33 (1897): 281-284.

    V. Pardington, Rayner S. "As Supplying a Need of Mixed City Life." *Homiletic Review* 33 (1897): 373-377.

    VI. Judson, Edward. "The Institutional Church a Remedy for Social Alienation." *Homiletic Review* 33 (1897): 472-476.

Taylor, William M. "Motives for a Forward Movement in Missionary Work." *Independent,* 27 March 1890, pp. 13, 14.

Tiffany, C.C. "The Church Congress at Detroit." *Independent,* 30 October 1884, p. 2.

Tinker, C.P. "Points Concerning Cornell Memorial." *Christian City* 11 (1899): 108.

———. "The Evangelistic Campaign at Cornell Memorial." *Christian City* 12 (1900): 46.

"The Church Congress." *American Church Review* 28 (1876): 156.

"The Church Congress." *Christian Union,* 28 November 1891, p. 1052.

"The Church Forsaking the Common People." *Independent,* 14 March 1895, p. 342.

"The City Wilderness." *Christian City* 11 (1899): 20, 21.

"The Five Points: A New Corner Stone." *Aggressive Methodism (Christian City)* 6 (1894): 5.

"The Institutional Idea in the Country." *Congregationalist,* 10 November 1892, p. 399.

"The Kindergarten Movement." *Outlook,* 1 April 1893, p. 601.

"The King's Daughters." *Presbyterian,* 30 July 1887, p. 11.

"The Moving Picture in the Sunday School." *Independent,* 31 July 1913, p. 277, 278.

"The Next Step for the Institutional Church." *Congregationalist,* 14 December 1893, p. 879.

Thompson, John Rhey. "Some Present Day Needs of Methodism, Especially in the Large Cities." *Christian City* 12 (1900): 55-57.

Thwing, Charles F. "A Mission to Business Men." *Independent,* 5 January 1888, p. 1.

Trevor, John. "The Labor Church: Religion of the Labor Movement." *Forum,* January 1895, pp. 597-601.

Tunis, John. "The Practical Treatment of the Problem of the Country Church." *Andover Review* 10 (1888): 221-232.

———. "Out of Town Missions for City Churches." *Andover Review* 12 (1889): 157-169.

Virgin, Samuel H. "The Christian Endeavor Movement." *Congregationalist,* 24 April 1890, p.2.

Wanamaker, John. "A Testimony to the Endeavor Movement." *Independent,* 7 July 1892, p. 929.

Ward, Harry F. "The Institutional Church." *Christian City* 12 (1900): 24-31.

Ward, Julius H. "Utility of the Church Congress." *American Church Review* 27 (1875): 56-65.

Wheelock, Lucy. "Kindergarten in the Sunday-school: A Protest." *Outlook,* 2 January 1892, pp. 20, 21.

Williams, Moseley H. "The New Era of Church Work in Philadelphia." *Open Church* 1 (1897): 53-74.

———. "The New Era of Church Work in Philadelphia: Second Article." *Open Church* 1 (1897): 107-121.

Winnington, Laura. "The Kitchen-Garden." *Outlook,* 4 May 1901, pp. 52, 53.

Winthrop, John. "Our Boston Letter." [Tremont Temple]. *Independent,* 28 February 1884, p. 5.

"What the Churches are Doing." *Independent,* 20 November 1913, p. 360.

"Young People's Movement in the Church: A Symposium." *Independent,* 7 July 1892, pp. 1-7.

Municipal Reform

"An Era of Municipal Reform." *Independent,* 17 January 1895.

"A Tale of Two Cities." *Christian City* 11 (1899): 82, 83.

Crafts, Wilbur F. "A Municipal Program: An Open Letter to the National Municipal League." *Christian City* 9 (1897): 264, 265.

Dunning, A.E. "A Campaign of Municipal Reform." *Congregationalist and Christian World,* 4 November 1905, p. 638.

Gates, Merrill E. "Municipal Reform and Tenement Houses." *Independent,* 10 January 1895, p. 38.

Kloss, Charles L. "The Civic Uprising in Philadelphia." *Congregationalist and Christian World,* 1 July 1905, pp. 18, 19.

"Municipal Progress." *Outlook,* 15 February 1896, p. 295.

"Municipal Reform." *Lutheran Observer,* 19 January 1894, p. 9.

"Municipal Reform." *Lutheran Observer,* 11 February 1898, p. 13.

"News of the Week: Domestic." *Independent,* 9 May 1895, p. 621.

Newton, R. Heber. "The People's Movement for Municipal Reform." *Independent,* 19 June 1890, p. 8.

Shinn, Charles H. "Needed Municipal Reform in San Francisco." *Outlook,* 11 July 1896, p. 53.

"The Month." *Aggressive Methodism (Christian City)* 6 (1894): 1, 2.

"Woman's Municipal League." *Outlook,* 18 May 1901, p. 140.

Zueblin, Charles. *A Decade of Civil Development.* Chicago: University of Chicago Press, 1905.

———. *American Municipal Progress: Chapters in Municipal Sociology.* New York: The Macmillan Co., 1902.

———. *Religion of a Democrat.* New York: B.W. Heubsch, 1908.

Pew Rents

Barringer, C.L. "Three Pews in the Church to Let." *Lutheran Observer,* 25 May 1894, p. 6.

Bridgman, Howard A. "A Plea for Free Pews." *Congregationalist,* 29 May 1890, p. 9.

Brokaw, Ralph W. "Pews Rented or Free—Which?" *Congregationalist,* 1 June 1893, p. 859.

Craik, James. "The Financial Question in the Church." *American Church Review* 38 (1882): 57-66.

Dana, M.M.G. "The Usher's Story." *Congregationalist,* 12 April 1882, p. 2.

"Facts about Pews: An Inside View of 36 Churches. Taxes, Rentals, Free Seats, Annual Deficits." *Congregationalist,* 13 February 1873, p. 3.

"Free and Open Church Association of the Protestant Episcopal Church." *Open Church* 2 (1898): 277, 278.

"Free Churches." *Congregationalist,* 20 February 1873, p. 1.

"Free Pews." *Presbyterian,* 24 January 1894, p. 9.

Hubbard, W.H. "The Pew System." *Congregationalist,* 16 February 1893, p. 256.

Langdon, Chauncy. "Reform in Church Finance." *American Church Review* 42 (1883): 364, 365.

Leavitt, George R. "Beware of Free Seats." *Congregationalist,* 1 May 1873, p. 2.

"List of Free Pew Churches." *Congregationalist,* 16 February 1893, p. 276.

McKenzie, Alexander. "Free Churches." *Congregationalist,* 12 December 1872, p. 1.

McKnight, George H. "Rental or Free, Which?" *Churchman,* 10 December 1892, p. 897.

Merriam, Charles. "Church Sittings." *Congregationalist,* 6 March 1873, p. 1.

Nesbit, D.K. "Some Advantages of the Pew Rent System." *Congregationalist,* 16 February 1893, pp. 255, 256.

North, Frank Mason. "In the Matter of Pew-Renting." *Christian Union,* 10 January 1889, p. 39.

Rice, Austin. "Western Need and Benevolence." *Congregationalist and Christan World,* 18 November 1905, p. 707.

" 'Stylus' and Free Seats." *Aggressive Methodism (Christian City)* 6 (1894): 7.

"The Free Pew System: Some of the Difficulties." *Christian Union,* 3 January 1889, p. 8.

"The Pewless Rich." *Christian Union,* 21 February 1889, p. 228.

" 'Up-Town' Churches." *Congregationalist,* 19 June 1873, p. 2.

Wasner, Samuel. "Another Aspect of the Financial Question in the Church." *American Church Review* 39 (1882): 20-30.

Protestant Social Thought

Barnett, Samuel. "The Church as Mediator between the Classes." *Independent,* 4 February 1892, pp. 153, 154.

Batten, Samuel Zane. "The Church as the Maker of Conscience." *American Journal of Sociology* 7 (1902): 611-628.

———. "Redemption of the Unfit." *American Journal of Sociology* 14 (1908): 233-260.

Beach, D.N. "Religion and University Life: The Experiment at Harvard." *Andover Review* 9 (1888): 597-604.

Behrends, A.J.F. "Symposium on the Pulpit: Is the Pulpit Declining in Power? If So, What is the Remedy? No. V." *Homiletic Review* 10 (1885): 376-383.

Bemis, Edward W. "Social Reforms Practicable and Otherwise." *Independent,* 15 April 1886, pp. 6, 7.

Berger, Peter L. and Neuhaus, Richard John, eds. *Against the World for the World: The Hartford Appeal and the Future of American Religion.* New York: Seabury Press, Crossroad Books, 1976.

Bradford, Amory H. "The Problem of Pauperism." *Andover Review* 13 (1890): 256-268.

Brinkerhoff, Roeliff. "Religion the Greatest Factor in Reform." *Lutheran Observer,* 14 January 1898, p. 1.

Buckely, James M. "Conference Sermon." *Proceedings of the Thirty-Third National Conference of Charities and Correction, Philadelphia, 1906,* pp. 11-18.

Carroll, H.K. "The Progress of Religion in the United States." New York *Christian Advocate,* 1 August 1895, pp. 491, 492.

Chandler, Joseph Haynes. "A Sign of the New Era." *Congregationalist,* 13 July 1893, pp. 47, 48.

Channing, William Ellery. "Address on Temperance at request of Council of Mass. Temperance Society, Odem, Boston, 28 February 1837." In *Works of William E. Channing, D.D.* 8th complete ed. 6 vols. Vol. 2, pp. 301-341. Boston, 1848.

"Church Life and Work: Are They On the Decline?" *Christian Union,* 6 April 1881, pp. 324-327.

"Church Work in Cities." *Christian Union,* 24 January 1889, p. 115.

Clark, Charles Worcester. "Applied Christianity: Who Shall Apply It First?" *Andover Review* 19 (1893): 18-33.

Cochrane, W.R. "Reasons for Plain Dressing at Church." *Congregationalist,* 25 September 1873, p. 2.

Crafts, Wilbur F. "The Gospel to the Poor." *Christian City* 12 (1900): 5, 6.

Delk, Edwin Heyl. "Civic Christianity." *Lutheran Quarterly* 23 (1893): 40-54.

———. "The Centrality of Christian Fellowship." *Lutheran Quarterly* 25 (1895): 527-540.

Denison, John Hopkins. "The Church the Mother of Progress." *Congregationalist and Christian World,* 21 October 1905, p. 551.

Dike, Samuel W. "The Religious Problem of the Country Town." *Andover Review* 2 (1884): 121-132; "The Religious Problem of the Country Town. II." *Andover Review* 3 (1885): 38-46; "The Religious Problem of the Country Town. III." *Andover Review* 3 (1885): 540-553; "The Religious Problem of the Country Town. IV." *Andover Review* 4 (1885): 191-208; "Suggestions on the Classification of Social Institutions." *Andover Review* 13 (1890): 677-684.

Dunham, M.E. "Our National Dangers." *Lutheran Observer,* 11 March 1898, pp. 2, 3.

Duryee, J.R. "The Christian Ministry of New York at the Beginning and End of the 19th Century." *Christian City* 10 (1898): 426-428.

Ecob, J.H. "University Extension: Church Extension." *Christian Union,* 28 November 1891, pp. 1030, 1032.

Ellwood, Charles A. "The Social Function of Religion." *American Journal of Sociology* 19 (1913): 289-307.

Everett, John Rutherford. *Religion in Economics.* New York: Morningside Heights, 1946.

Fairchild, E.M. "The Function of the Church." *American Journal of Sociology* 2 (1896): 220-233.

Fisher, John Alonzo. "John Hopkins University and Christianity." *Independent,* 6 November 1884, p. 6.

"Fitting New Conditions." Congregationalist, 13 July 1893, p. 41.

"Gospel of Wealth." *Outlook,* 9 March 1901, p. 571.

Graif, Philip. "The Clergyman: Is He a Social Parasite?" *Lutheran Observer,* 1 June 1894, p. 2.

Hall, John. "The Christian Workers." *Independent,* 18 November 1886, pp. 1, 2.

Hesselgrave, Charles E. "The Failure of Smith: The Church Is Not the Only Thing the Average Man Neglects." *Independent,* 29 May 1913, pp. 1184-1187.

Hoadley, James H. "The Gospel and the Poor." *Independent,* 26 April 1888, pp. 2, 3.

Hoben, Allan. "American Democracy and the Modern Church." *American Journal of Sociology* 21 (1916): 458-473.

———. "American Democracy and the Modern Church. II." *American Journal of Sociology* 22 (1917): 489-502.

"How to Do It." *Lutheran Observer,* 3 January 1890, p. 2.

Huntington, Frederic Dan. "Morality and Public Education." *Independent,* 17 January 1888, p. 3.

"In and About Chicago." *Christian Union,* 28 February 1889, p. 262.

Jackson, Alexander. "The Relation of the Classes to the Church." *Independent,* 1 March 1888, p. 2, 3.

Jordan, David Starr. "Sources of National Degradation." *Lutheran Observer,* 29 June 1894, p. 1.

Kinley, David. "The Law of Social Progress." New York *Christian Advocate,* 17 August 1893, pp. 527, 538.

———. "The Relation of Social Reform to Social Evolution." New York *Christian Advocate,* 24 August 1893, pp. 543, 544.

———. "Some Tendencies in Social Reform." New York *Christian Advocate,* 31 August 1893, pp. 554, 555.

———. "The Relation of the Church to Social Reform." New York *Christian Advocate,* 7 September 1893, pp. 575, 576.

Laidlaw, Walter. "The Church and the City Community." *American Journal of Sociology* 6 (1911): 794-804.

Loomis, Samuel Lane. "The Growth of Modern Cities." *Andover Review* 7 (1887): 341-358.

———. "The Social Composition of American Cities." *Andover Review* 7 (1887): 475-491.

———. "Christian Work in London." *Andover Review* 7 (1887): 592-606.

———. "Christian Work in London. II. Dissenting Churches, Other Movements." *Andover Review* 8 (1887): 16-31.

Low, Seth. "The City University." *Independent,* 2 August 1894, pp. 2, 3.

Macarthur, Robert Stuart. "Applied Christianity." *Lutheran Observer,* 2 March 1894, p. 1.

McGlynn, Edward. "Justice Wanted More than Charity." *Independent,* 11 December 1890, p. 3.

Meredith, Irving. "American Institute of Christian Sociology." *Congregationalist,* 27 July 1893, p. 134.

Methodist Federation for Social Service. *The Church and the Social Question: The Declaration of the General Conference of 1916 and Sections of the Episcopal Addresses of 1912 and 1916.* Chicago. Newberry Library. Graham Taylor Collection.

"Methodist Philanthropy." *Christian City* 11 (1899): 115.

Miller, E. "The Pastor for the Times." *Lutheran Quarterly* 23 (1893): 173-193.

Munger, Theodore T. "Then and Now." *Independent,* 29 May 1894, p. 4.

———. "Recent Changes in Christian Thought." *Outlook,* 27 February 1892, pp. 410, 411.

North, Louise M. "The Science and the Grace of Charity." *Aggressive Methodism (Christian City)* 6 (1894): 3, 4.

Park, C.W. "The Free Religious Association." *Congregationalist,* 21 June 1882, p. 2.

"Pauper Children of a Rich City." *Christian City* 11 (1899): 136.

Peabody, A.P. "Wealth." *Andover Review* 19 (1893): 321-337.

Phelps, William Lyon. "Confessions of a Baptist." *Independent,* 14 May 1908, pp. 1084-1086.

Post, T.M. "Transition Periods in Religious Thought." *Andover Review* 1 (1884): 577-594.

"Poverty a Blessing." *Lutheran Observer,* 31 January 1890, p. 7.

Raymond, Bradford P. "The Church and Patriotism." *Christian City* 10 (1898): 432, 433.

Richards, Charles H. "Christian Thought and Service in Our Day." *Congregationalist,* 1 May 1890, p.9.

Riegler, Gordon A. *Socialization of the New England Clergy, 1800-1860.* Greenfield, Ohio: The Greenfield Printing & Publishing Co., 1945.

"Religion and Cities." New York *Christian Advocate,* 7 March 1895, p. 151.

"Religiosity and Religion." *Independent,* 9 April 1908, pp. 812, 813.

Robinson, Willard H. "Social Reforms or Jesus—Which?" *Independent,* 23 August 1894, pp. 2, 3.

Rylance, J.H. *Lectures on Social Questions.* New York: Thomas Whittaker, 1880.

"Salvation Social." *Independent,* 27 October 1910, pp. 937, 938.

Sanborn, Alvan F. "The Anatomy of a Tenement Street." *Forum,* January 1895, pp. 554-572.

Scudder, Vida D. "Socialism and Spiritual Progress." *Andover Review* 16 (1891): 49-67.

Sheers, William. "Election to Service." *Christian City* 12 (1900): 81, 82.

Sheldon, Charles M. "The Great Catastrophe of 1913." *Independent,* 30 January 1913, pp. 232-236.

"Side Lights." [League for Social Service]. *Christian City* 11 (1899): 115.

Smith, Homer J. "Who Shall Save Our Cities?" New York *Christian Advocate,* 3 October 1895, pp. 635, 636.

Smith, Willard H. "William Jennings Bryan and the Social Gospel." *Journal of American History* 53 (1906): 41-59.

Smyth, Egbert C. "The Theological Purpose of the Review." *Andover Review* 1 (1884): 1-13.

Smyth, Newman. "Christian Economics." *Independent,* 3 January 1884, p. 3.

———. "Social Problems in the Pulpit." "Sermon I. Claims of Labor." *Andover Review* 3 (1885): 302-312; "Sermon II. Use and Abuse of Capital." *Andover Review* 3 (1885): 423-436; "Sermon III. Social Helps." *Andover Review* 3 (1885): 508-519.

"Socialism and Religion." *Independent,* 12 June 1908, p. 1360.

"Social Reforms." New York *Christian Advocate,* 17 January 1895, p. 33.

Spargo, John. "Christian Socialism in America." *American Journal of Sociology* 15 (1909): 16-20.

Stelzle, Charles. "Social and Religious Conditions in Leading American Cities." Louisville *Christian Observer,* 8 May 1912, p. 439.

————. "The Church as a Social Agency." Louisville *Christian Observer,* 6 November 1912, p. 1098.

————. "The Church a Social Force." Louisville *Christian Observer,* 13 November 1912, p. 1114.

————. "The Churches in a Unified Program of Advance." Louisville *Christian Observer,* 20 November 1912, p. 1151.

Sterrett, J. Macbride. "Sociology in the West." *Churchman,* 26 March 1892, pp. 377, 378.

"Symposium on Wealth and Christianity."

   James, D. Willis. "How Wealth Should Be Given." *Independent,* 7 January 1892, pp. 1, 2.

   Ogden, Robert C. "Money and Christianity." *Independent,* 7 January 1892, p. 2.

   Gates, Merrill E. "The Christian's Dilemma as to Accumulation." *Independent,* 7 January 1892, pp. 2, 3.

   Buckley, James M. "The Proper Uses of Christian Wealth." *Independent,* 7 January 1892, p. 3.

   Macarthur, Robert S. "The Right Use of Wealth." *Independent,* 7 January 1892, pp. 3, 4.

   Ellinwood, F.E., "The Meaning of Wealth in Christian Hands." *Independent,* 7 January 1892, p. 5.

"The Cause of Their Poverty." *Lutheran Observer,* 30 March 1894, p. 11.

"The Christian's Work." *Lutheran Observer,* 2 March 1894, p. 2.

"The Church and Human Interests." *Congregationalist and Christian World,* 8 July 1905, p. 44.

"The Church and Social Work." *Proceedings of the Thirty-eighth National Conference of Charities and Correction, Boston, 1911.*

   White, William J. "The Catholic Church and Social Work." pp. 221-225.

   Crothers, Samuel McChord. "The Church and Social Work." pp. 225-229.

   Hall, Frank Oliver. "The Influence of the Church." pp. 229-233.

   Stelzle, Charles. "The Preparation of Ministers for Social Work. (a) The Preparation in the Seminary." pp. 233-237.

   North, Frank Mason. "The Preparation of Ministers for Social Work. (b) The Preparation in Life." pp. 237-243.

   Holmes, Samuel Van Vranken. "What the Church Can Do as an Organization in Lines of Social Work." pp. 244-249.

   Melish, John Howard. "How the Church Can Help Other Organizations." pp. 249-255.

   Almy, Frederic. "The Value of the Church to Social Workers." pp. 255-259.

"The Church Congress on Socialism." *Christian Union,* 28 November 1891, pp. 1024, 1025.

"The Consecration of Wealth." *Congregationalist,* 17 April 1890, p. 4.

"The Standard of Human Worth." *Independent,* 1 June 1905, pp. 1261-1263.

The Socialized Church. Addresses of conference of Methodist social workers, November 1908. New York: Eaton & Mains, 1910.

"The Undeserving Poor." *Independent,* 13 February 1908: 376, 377.

"The Unemployed." *Independent,* 5 March 1908, pp. 537, 538.

"The Unification of Humanity." *Independent,* 5 March 1908, pp. 538, 539.

"These Hard Times." *Congregationalist,* 20 March 1878, p. 4.

Thrall, J. Brainard. "The Minister's Vocation and Advocation." *Andover Review* 2 (1884): 145-147.

Thwing, Charles F. "How Much Shall I Give?" *Congregationalist,* 13 December 1882, p. 2.

Valentine, M. "Reaching Our Non-Christian Population." *Lutheran Observer,* 7 February 1890, p. 1.

Vaughan, Bernard. *Socialism from the Christian Standpoint.* New York: The Macmillan Co., 1912.

Washburn, William Ives. "The Layman's Part in Mission Work." *Congregationalist,* 15 May 1890, p. 9.

Weigle, E.D. "The Ministry and Current Social Problems." *Lutheran Quarterly* 24 (1894): 467-480.

Welch, Herbert. "The Relation of the Church to the Social Worker." In *Proceedings of the Thirty-fifth National Conference of Charities and Correction, Richmond, 1908,* pp. 69-75.

"What It Costs to Maintain Christianity." *Outlook,* 26 January 1901, p. 195.

Whiteing, Richard. *No. 5 John Street.* New York: The Century Co., 1899.

Wilson, Warren H. "The Church and the Rural Community." *American Journal of Sociology* 16 (1911): 668-702.

Wright, O.A. "The Saloon and the City." *Christian City* 10 (1898): 772, 773.

Wynn, W.H. "The Sacred and Secular." *Lutheran Observer,* 29 November 1889, p. 1.

Settlements

"A Methodist Church Settlement on the East Side." *Christian City* 12 (1900): 75.

Atterbury, Anson P. "The Church Settlement." *Open Church* 1 (1897): 161-173.

"Christodora House." *Christian City* 12 (1900): 31-33.

Church Settlement House. *Report.* January 1897. Chicago. Newberry Library. Graham Taylor Collection.

East Side House. *Fourth Annual Report for the Year Ending 31 December 1895.* Chicago. Newberry Library, Graham Taylor Collection.

"Epiphany House, Stanton Street, New York." *Churchman,* 5 November 1892, p. 608.

Gavit, John Palmer, ed. *Bibliography of College, Social and University Settlements.* 3rd ed., rev. Compiled for the College Settlements Association. Cambridge, Mass.: Co-operative Press, 1897.

Gavit, John Palmer. "Story of Chicago Commons." *Christian City* 11 (1899): 84-87.

Kildare, Owen. "The Slums' Point of View." *Independent,* 22 June 1905, pp. 1394-1399.

McCulloch, James E. *The Mastery of Love: A Narrative of Settlement Life.* New York: Fleming H. Revell Co., 1910.

North, Frank Mason. "Church Settlements." *Open Church* 1 (1897): 103.

"Religious Aspect of Social Settlements." *Churchman,* 27 February 1897, p. 308.

"The Epworth League House, Boston." *Open Church* 2 (1898): 353, 354.

Urban Evangelism

Crafts, Wilbur F. "The Supreme Importance of City Evangelization." *Independent,* 24 September 1884, p.1.

Dixon, Thomas. *Failure of Protestantism in New York and Its Causes.* 2nd ed. New York: Strauss & Rehn Publishing Co., 1896.

Francis, John Junkin. "Great Evangelistic Movement in Cincinnati." *Independent,* 11 Febraury 1892, p. 204.

Hall, Charles Cuthbert. "The Motive of City Evangelization." *Christian City* 11 (1899): 55-57.

Johnson, John Edgar. "Evangelistic Work in Our Great Cities." *Christian Union,* 3 January 1889, p. 17.

Johnston, John Wesley. "Abide in Your Cities." *Christian City* 10 (1898): 383.

Loomis, Samuel Lane. "Protestant Evangelism: Methods Employed by the Rev. B. Fay Mills." *Independent,* 5 June 1890, pp. 1, 2.

"Methodist City Missions." *Outlook,* 11 July 1896, p. 65.

North, Crandall J. "The Twentieth Century Movement in New Haven." *Christian City* 11 (1899): 73, 74.

Pentecost, George F. "Evangelization of Our Cities. No. I." *Homiletic Review* 10 (1885): 291-299.

———. "Evangelization of Our Cities. No. II." *Homiletic Review* 10 (1885): 392-404.

———. "Evangelization of Our Cities. No. III." *Homiletic Review* 10 (1885): 474-481.

———. "The Relation of the Congregational Churches to the Work of Evangelism." *Independent,* 4 November 1886, pp. 14-17.

Rood, Henry. "Men and Religion." *Independent,* 21 December 1911, pp. 1362-1366.

"Sam Small and Sam Jones in Baltimore." *Independent,* 20 May 1886, p. 13.

Sheridan, Wilbur F. "Detroit's Forward Movement." *Aggressive Methodism (Christian City)* 6 (1894): 10.

Sproull, J.W. "City Evangelization in Pittsburgh." *Independent,* 20 May 1886, p. 14.

"The 'Two Sams' in Chicago." *Independent,* 18 March 1886, p. 13.

"The Work in the North End Mission." *Congregationalist,* 20 March 1873, p. 1.

Traveller, A.D. "Chicago: A Splendid Record." *Aggressive Methodism (Christian City)* 6 (1894): 3.

"Young People's Forward Movement." *Congregationalist and Christian World,* 12 August 1905, p. 228.

Background and General Material

Abell, Aaron Ignatius. *The Urban Impact on American Protestantism, 1865-1900.* Hamden: Archon, 1962.

Bettman, Otto L. *The Good Old Days—They Were Terrible!* New York: Random House, 1974.

Buckham, John Wright. *Progressive Religious Thought in America: A Survey of the Enlarging Pilgrim Faith.* Boston: Houghton, Mifflin & Co., 1919.

Carter, Paul A. *Decline and Revival of the Social Gospel: Social and Political Liberalism in American Protestant Churches, 1920-1940.* Ithica: Cornell University Press, 1954.

Cheney, Mary Bushnell, ed. *Life and Letters of Horace Bushnell.* New York: Harper & Bros., 1880.

Cresebrough, A.S. "The Theological Opinions of Horace Bushnell as Related to His Character and Christian Experience." *Andover Review* 6 (1886): 113-130.

Dombrowski, James. *The Early Days of Christian Socialism in America.* New York: Columbia University Press, 1936.

Forward Movements—containing Brief Statements regarding Institutional Churches, Social Settlements, Rescue Missions. Congregational Handbook Series. Boston: W.L. Green & Co., 1894.

Fremantle, William Henry. *The World as the Subject of the Redemption, being an Attempt to Set Forth the Functions of the Church as Designed to Embrace the Whole Race of Mankind.* The Bampton Lectures, delivered before the University of Oxford in 1883. 2nd ed., rev. With an introduction by Richard T. Ely. New York: Longmans, Green & Co., 1895.

Gaustad, Edwin Scott. *A Religious History of America.* New York: Harper & Row, 1966.

Goldman, Eric F. *Rendezvous with Destiny.* New York: Random House, Vintage Books, 1956.

Griffin, Clifford S. *Their Brothers' Keepers: Moral Stewardship in the United States, 1800-1865.* New Brunswick: Rutgers University Press, 1960.

Hart, James D. "Platitudes of Piety: Religion and the Popular Modern Novel." *American Quarterly* 6 (1954): 311-322.

Hofstadter, Richard. *The Age of Reform.* New York: Random House, Vintage Books, 1955.

Hopkins, Charles Howard. *The Rise of the Social Gospel in American Protestantism.* New Haven: Yale University Press, 1940.

Hughes, Hugh Price. *Social Christianity: Sermons Delivered in St. James's Hall, London.* New York: Funk & Wagnalls, 1895.

King, Bolton. *Mazzini.* The Temple Biographies. New York: E.P. Dutton & Co., 1902.

May, Henry F. *Protestant Churches and Industrial America.* New York: Octagon Books, 1949. Reprint, 1963.

McLoughlin, William G. *Modern Revivalism: Charles Grandison Finney to Billy Graham.* New York: Ronald Press Co., 1959.

Miller, Perry. *The Life of the Mind in America: From the Revolution to the Civil War.* New York: Harcourt, Brace & World, 1965.

Morgan, Edmund S. *Visible Saints: The History of a Puritan Idea.* New York: New York University Press, 1963.

Morris, Lloyd R. *Incredible New York: High Life and Low Life of the Last Hundred Years.* New York: Random House, 1951.

Nash, Henry S. *Genesis of the Social Conscience: The Relation between the Establishment of Christianity in Europe and the Social Question.* New York: The Macmillan Co., 1897.

———. *Ethics and Revelation.* New York: The Macmillan Co., 1899.

Newcomb, Simon. "A Plain Man's Talk on the Labor Question." Series in various issues of the *Independent,* 1886.

Nicholl, Grier. "The Christian Social Novel in America, 1865-1918." Ph.D. dissertation, University of Minnesota, 1964.

Potter, Henry C. *Sermons of the City.* New York: E.P. Dutton & Co., 1881.

Rovere, Richard H. *The Magnificent Shysters: The True and Scandalous History of Howe & Hummel.* New York: Grosset & Dunlap, 1947.

Russell Sage Foundation. *The Inter-Relation of Social Movements with Information about 67 Organizations.* Published by the Charity Organization Department of the Russell Sage Foundation. New York, 1910.

Singmaster, J.A. "The Lutheran Church in New York City." *Lutheran Observer,* 3 January 1890, p. 2.

Skardon, Alvin W. *Church Leader in the Cities: William Augustus Muhlenberg.* Philadelphia: University of Pennsylvania Press, 1971.

Small, Albion W. "The Meaning of the Social Movement." *American Journal of Sociology* 3 (1897): 340-354.

Spargo, John. *The Spiritual Significance of Modern Socialism.* New York: B.W. Huebsch, 1908.

Talmage, Thomas DeWitt. *Social Dynamite: Or, the Wickedness of Modern Society.* Chicago: Standard Publishing Co., 1888.

"The Five Points of Calvinism." *Congregationalist,* 30 August 1882, p. 4.

Troeltsch, Ernst. *Protestantism and Progress.* Translated by W. Montgomery. New York: G.P. Putnam's Sons, 1913.

Vissert t 'Hooft, Willem A. *The Background of the Social Gospel in America.* Haarlem: H.D. Tjeenk Willink & Zoon, 1928. Reprint. St. Louis: Bethany Press, n.d.

Werner, Morris, Robert. *It Happened in New York.* New York: Coward-McCann, 1957.

Workingman's Advocate. Official organ of the National Labor Union. Issued weekly. Chicago and Cincinnati. Vols. 7-12. April 1871 to June 1877.

EPILOGUE:
Protestant Social Welfare Thought

American Protestantism as represented in the institutional churches, the settlements, and the organized charities of the 1890s and the early twentieth century was "the Social Gospel of the center, where the main strength of the movement lay." It was not the reordering of the antislavery impulse that manifested itself again after the Civil War in such crusades as the temperance movement, or in the "humbler patterns" of rescue missions and the Salvation Army. It was far more evangelical than the secularized YMCA. It steered away from the liberal and radical socialism of William Dwight Porter Bliss and George D. Herron. Neither was it simply a response to critical urban problems brought by rapid urbanization and immigration—such as poverty, disease, overcrowding in slums, and unemployment. It was, rather, the dedicated and active search of middle-class Protestants of many denominations for a Christian America; and their attempts to mold what Lutheran sociologist J.H.W. Stuckenberg called a "distinct" nationality—" a nationality in which the people, the whole people, reign; but under God, subject to His law."[1]

It was in relation to this goal that Protestant clergymen spoke of "Christianizing the social order," of recognizing a "higher law," or of "the incarnation of the golden rule in civic and social life." As a Lutheran clergyman expressed it, "A nation's religion is the chief fact in regard to it. . . . Without religion it will and must dissolve into its original elements and end in anarchy. . . . This is not equivalent to saying that it must have a theology or a creed incorporated into its constitution. But it must think religiously, that it may act religiously. It must have a conscience, . . . a national perception of eternal truth." Protestant progressives saw the precepts of the New Testament as providing the substance that would develop true patriotism and fill up with spiritual content the mere forms of rights and privileges guaranteed by law.[2]

There thus developed among responsible leaders of the Social Gospel of the center a body of social welfare thought that was both religious and uniquely American. It was sprinkled about in the writings, speeches, and public utterances of institutional churchmen, both clergy and lay. It was given eloquent expression in the activities of free and open churches and Christian settlements. It sprang from the indigenous roots of Horace Bushnell, drew upon the democratic philosophy of Joseph Mazzini, and embodied the Chatauqua idea of "education for everybody, everywhere, and in every department of knowledge." It extolled America as "the Nation of God's Right Hand"; it saw the state as "the representative of the divine power and the divine goodness"; it taught that the evils of American society could be remedied "only by the co-operation of religious teaching and direct legislation."[3]

Protestant progressives equated American democracy with Christianity. They believed that Jesus Christ came into the world "to promote human welfare" and "to inaugurate democracy." They envisioned, and sought to construct, a Christian commonwealth. In the beginning, they sought to achieve their goal by changing the nation's "organized competitive life" into an "organic co-operative life," through voluntary means. They saw cooperation, federation, and fraternalism as natural aspects of humanity that could be developed and channeled to bring about a Christian democratic America. They considered reciprocity to be "God's law for society," and they considered society to consist of "exactly balanced rights and duties." The more idealistic among them, such as institutional church pastors Edward Judson and James O.S. Huntington, sought to recapture "the glory and miracle of the primitive church" by creating a church society "in which human units can cohere on a common plane—rich and poor, prince and pauper, the learned and the illiterate." The more practical among them, such as university professors William Jewett Tucker and Richard T. Ely, concentrated on economic or business life and stressed the ordinary day-by-day relationships among people. Ely advocated "voluntary associations to unite labor and capital in the same hands"; and Tucker emphasized that the "Christian motive" could be made influential through "the conduct of business, the treatment of employees and domestic servants, the discharge of service for wages, the exercise of hospitality, the use of social leadership."[4]

In the late nineteenth century, the "great and increasing body of chronic wretchedness" that socially minded Protestants saw everywhere about them in urban America led them to give serious attention to such political schemes as socialism and Edward Bellamy's nationalism, and to try to come to grips with such secular philosophies as Social Darwinism. A number of leading Protestant progressives were very sympathetic to socialism. At the turn of the century, University of Chicago theologian Shailer Mathews noted that "socialism and Christianity are alike in that they are both laboring for a new and higher social order, in which all . . . shall live better and happier lives." In 1901, liberal journalist Lyman Abbott wrote that the labor unions and the strikes revealed the "true meaning" of socialism—seeking "to secure the world for all and put it truly under the control of all." Even as late as 1913, Harvard University philosopher Francis Greenwood Peabody described Marxism as "not an expression of economic determinism but an expression of human determination."[5]

In the end, however, Protestants of the Social Gospel of the center rejected political socialism because of its materialistic conception of human needs, its tendency toward anarchy—and, most of all, because of its menace to individual liberty. Protestant progressives also concluded that Darwinism, in its emphasis upon "the struggle for life," ignored the essential Christian motive of "the struggle for life of others." They noted that "mutual aid is a higher law than the survival of the strongest," and that "the survival of the fittest" is not necessarily "the survival of the best." They were looking toward a socialistic state where "material wealth will be distributed on the basis, not of service, but of need."[6]

Protestant progressives resolved their ambivalent struggle with socialism by applying to it a Darwinian gradualism that toned down the idea of socialism "until it meant little more than the vague organic unity of the race." They all agreed that "we have no fixed theory against socialism, for we are moving that way, and we do not know where we shall stop." They dismissed the problem, however, as "a pure question of political economy, which a future generation must solve." They put "all the emphasis" upon gradualism, so that Christian socialism came to be only a method, with the social goal "all but lost to view."[7]

Perhaps a fairer critique of Protestant progressivism lies, however, not in its philosophical flirtation with socialism but in its real grappling with the question of the proper relation of church and state in a Christian commonwealth. In their efforts to democratize their churches, and through their churches to democratize America, Protestant churchmen became involved in social problems of such massive proportions that they came to believe that the state, as well as the church, had a necessary social function to perform—that neither church nor state could solve the problems alone. Even in the 1870s, early Protestant progressives had occasionally voiced opinions about the welfare role of the state in general, and about American forms of government in particular. In 1876, for example, a Protestant clergyman had called the church "needy—all but a mendicant in this land," and had suggested that the "strong" material resources of the state were needed "in the ministry of alms-giving."[8]

In 1891, in a series of monthly articles in the New York *Christian Advocate,* Episcopalian economist Richard T. Ely wrote that the possiblities of private philanthropy had been exaggerated, that "social reforms must be accomplished chiefly by established, regularly-working institutions, served by individual effort and strengthened by private philanthropy." He lamented the fact that "laws are chiefly negative, repressive, and mandatory, whereas they ought to be attractive and persuasive as well." He believed that the law must be transformed, "giving it a more Christian character."[9]

In 1901, liberal editor Lyman Abbott wrote in the *Outlook* that the function of government was to protect every man "in his person, property, reputation, family, and liberties," and that if the government oppresses the weak, "it no longer has authority." He declared that suffrage, or "participation in government," was not a right, but only one means to the preservation of rights. "The existing government," he said, determines the rights to be protected, and the method of protecting them, since "whoever possesses power is, by the mere possession, . . . responsible for its right employment."[10]

Of all the Protestant progressives, economist John R. Commons and Baptist theologian Walter Rauschenbusch were by far the most astutely perceptive of the emerging nature of American democracy. Commons gave particular attention to the place of politics in American life. He cautioned that the important questions of his day were socio-economic questions rather than political questions, but he agreed that politics was "the most manifold and far-reaching activity open to the American citizen" and "the principal means by which institutions are shaped and modified." He described proper politics as involving the "right kind of laws," the "right kind of men," and the "right kind of voluntary co-operation with officials."[11]

Both Commons and Rauschenbusch foresaw the interest-group nature of the democracy that was to take permanent form in the United States by the end of the 1930s. Commons remarked that "good in politics is accomplished only by moving massive bodies." Rauschenbusch declared that "a given truth" must depend "for a definite historical victory" upon some "great and conquering class whose self-interest is bound up with the victory of that principle."[12]

By 1907, Rauschenbusch had correctly noted the relationship between wealth and political power in America. In his *Christianity and the Social Crisis* he wrote that "if a class arrives at economic wealth, it will gain political influence and some form of representation," and that "a class which controls legislation will shape it for its own enrichment." He believed that "social equality can coexist with the greatest of natural differences," but noted that, in America, even though all were equal before the law "in theory," the right of appeal gave tremendous odds to those with "financial staying power." He concluded that "we cannot join economic inequality and political equality," that "if we want approximate political equality, we must have approximate economic equality."[13]

In 1885, Joseph Cook, whose "Boston Monday Lectures" of 1875-1880 had made his name "a household word in orthodox circles, whether he dealth with biology, labor, transcendentalism, heredity, or socialism," had written that "in a good and great cause the people are invincible and ought to be." He declared that "what the people greatly desire they will ultimately achieve under American forms of government." Well before the end of the century, however, the enthusiastic and simplistic belief in the welfare "invincibility" of the American people that had been expressed by Cook began to fade. Mathews spoke of "unemployed reformers," and Protestant churches began to make conscious efforts to shift the welfare burden to government and to define a concept of legal welfare rights.[14]

The First World War brought disillusionment to all peace-loving American democrats. By 1920, "progressive politics had been virtually swept from the stage"; and in the era of "normalcy" the middle class, including the Protestant church membership, for the most part bid "farewell to reform." Yet, throughout the 1920s, denominational weeklies were filled with "articulate and vigorous social criticism"; and "the forthright labor gospel of Rauschenbusch and Gladden" continued to be a factor in American Protestantism.[15]

Guided by their "social creed" of 1912, the federated Protestant churches continued to see themselves as "something more than one among many social institutions," as "society's priest—that which mediates God to a race that can but does not worship." The 1912 platform of the Federal Council of the Churches of Christ was revised in 1928; and the 1930s saw a new rise of the Social Gospel, marked by the publication of Reinhold Niebuhr's *Moral Man and Immoral Society* in 1932, by the establishment of a Fellowship of Socialist Christians, and by a strong ecumenical thrust that was worldwide.[16]

Even more important, the Social Question of the Protestant progressives—how to reconcile the individual personality with an evolutionary industrial order; how to explain wealth and poverty in an industrial society, and how to eradicate them; and how to relate industrial competition and social inequality to democracy and the Christian ethic—has remained unsolved in twentieth century America. The disease, the poverty, and the uncertainty of daily life in American cities, on the one hand—coupled with bossism and the rise of corporate financial and political power on the other hand—led progressive Protestants, as well as secular sociologists and others, to frame the Social Question as follows: How can a heterogeneous society endure, and still be *free and democratic,* with actual legal and economic equality for all?

Walter Rauschenbusch was greatly troubled in 1907 by the disturbing presence in America of "a rich class and a poor class, whose manner of life is wedged farther and farther apart, and whose boundary lines are becoming ever more distinct." In the 1970s a middle-class America—a Protestant America—again became troubled by this disturbing presence and once more raised the Social Question. The fact that it has never been answered gives the social welfare thought of the progressive Christianity of the late nineteenth and early twentieth centuries a stature and a permanent relevance that cannot be lightly dismissed.[17]

NOTES

1. The analysis of the Social Gospel used here is that found in Paul A. Carter, *Decline and Revival of the Social Gospel: Social and Political Liberalism in American Protestant Churches, 1920-1940* (New York, 1954), pp. 12-16. For a thorough and reliable treatment of W.D.P. Bliss and George D. Herron, see Charles Howard Hopkins, *Rise of the Social Gospel in American Protestantism, 1865-1915* (New Haven, 1940), pp. 173-200. Aaron A. Abell discusses the history of the YMCA and YWCA, temperance organizations and city missions, and the Salvation Army in his *Urban Impact on American Protestantism, 1865-1900* (Hamden, 1962), pp. 27-56, 118-136. The quotations are from Carter, *Decline and Revival of the Social Gospel*, pp. 15, 12; and J.H.W. Stuckenberg, "Proper Use of National Blessings the Best Evidence of Gratitude," *Homiletic Review* 8 (1884): 865.

2. The quotations are from Edwin Heyl Delk, "Civic Christianity," *Lutheran Quarterly* 23 (1893): 40-44; John Hall, "Need for Christian Effort," *Independent*, 21 Oct. 1890; and Bradford P. Raymond, "The Church and Patriotism," *Christian City* 10 (1898): 433.

3. The quotations are from Jesse L. Hurlbut, *Story of Chautauqua* (New York, 1921), p. 27; John Reid Shannon, "The Nation of God's Right Hand," New York *Christian Advocate*, 4 July 1885; Washington Gladden, "What to Do with the Workless Man," *Proceedings of the Twenty-sixth National Conference of Charities and Correction* (1899), p. 149 (hereafter cited as *Proceedings*); and Jaspar W. Gilbert, "Lay Criticism on the Ministry and the Methods of Church Work. No. XI," *Homiletic Review* 12 (1885): 216.

4. The quotations are from Lyman Abbott, "Christianity and Democracy," *Outlook*, 11 Jan. 1896; Walter Rauschenbusch, "Ideals of Social Reformers," *American Journal of Sociology* 2 (1896): 210; M.W. Stryker, "Rights and Duties of Craft and Capital," *Independent*, 2 May 1895; Judson, "Symposium on the Institutional Church. VI. The Institutional Church a Remedy for Social Alienation," *Homiletic Review* 33 (1897): 472; Richard T. Ely, "Co-operation in America: In Five Articles. No. 1. Relation of Co-operation to Other Phases of the American Labor Movement," *Congregationalist*, 11 Feb. 1886; and Tucker, "Christianity and Its Modern Competitors. II. Social Ethics, *Andover Review* 7 (1887): 76.

5. The quotations are from Walter Rauschenbusch, *Christianity and the Social Crisis*, Harper Torchbook Edition (1964, edited by Robert D. Cross from New York, 1907), p. 246; Mathews, "The Church and the Social Movement," *American Journal of Sociology* 4 (1899): 614-616; Abbott, "The Rights of Man: A Study in Twentieth Century Problems. VI. The Industrial Rights of Man," *Outlook*, 11 May 1901; and Peabody, "Socialization of Religion," *American Journal of Sociology* 18 (1913): 702.

6. The quotations are from Samuel Zane Batten, "Redemption of the Unfit," *American Journal of Sociology* 14 (1908): 234; Charles Worcester Clark, "Applied Christianity: Who Shall Apply It First? *Andover Review* 19 (1893): 33; David Starr Jordan, "Sources of National Degradation," *Lutheran Observer*, 29 June 1984; and Vida D. Scudder, "Socialism and Spirtual Progress—A Speculation," *Andover Review* 16 (1891): 49, 50.

7. The quotations are from James Dombrowski, *Early Days of Christian Socialism in America* (New York, 1936), p. 26; and "Socialism and Religion," *Independent*, 11 June 1908.

8. F.D. Hoskins, "Pauperism and Its Treatment," *American Church Review* 31 (1897): 141.

9. The quotations are taken from the ten articles by Richard T. Ely entitled "Suggestions on Social Topics," in various issues of the New York *Christian Advocate*, beginning with 12 Feb. 1891 and ending with 3 Dec. 1891.

10. Abbott, "The Rights of Man: A Study in Twentieth Century Problems. V. Law and Liberty," *Outlook*, 4 May 1901.

11. Commons, *Social Reform and the Church* (New York, 1894), pp. 53, vi; idem, "Social Economics and City Evangelization," *Christian City* 10 (1898): 770.

12. Commons, *Social Reform and the Church*, p. 52; and Rauschenbusch, *Christianity and the Social Crisis*, pp. 401, 402.

13. Rauschenbusch, *Christianity and the Social Crisis*, pp. 247-264.

14. The quotations are from Hopkins, *Rise of the Social Gospel*, p. 40; Cook, "Symposium on Prohibition: Ought Prohibition to Be Made a Political Question: If So with What Limitations? No. IV," *Homiletic Review* 10 (1885): 286, 287; and Mathews, "The Church and the Social Movement," 611.

15. Carter, *Decline and Revival of the Social Gospel*, pp. 18-22, 67.

16. Mathews, "The Christian Church and the Social Unity," 467; and Carter, *Decline and Revival of the Social Gospel*, pp. 141-156, 183-188.

17. The quotation is from Rauschenbusch, *Christianity and the Social Crisis*. p. 249.

1460 Bramble Ct
Rio Rancho NM 87124